Earthships

A New Mecca Poetry

Collection

Earthships,

A New Mecca Poetry Collection copyright © 2007

Editors:

Zachary Kluckman

Jessica Helen Lopez

ISBN: 978-0-6151-4418-4

Front cover painting copyright © B. Joseph McQueen
http:www.highbelow.com

Back cover painting copyright © Bill Gambling

Cover design and interior layout by Zachary Kluckman

Horse and Tiger Press
c/o NM Poetry Tangents
23 Longview Drive
Tijeras, NM 87059

Earthships:
A New Mecca Poetry
Collection

Edited by:

Zachary Kluckman
Jessica Helen Lopez

Horse and Tiger Press : : Albuquerque

Acknowledgements

"When It Rains" by Carol Moldaw originally appeared in *Taken from the River* (Alef Books, 1993). Reprinted by permission of the artist. All rights reserved.

"*The North Window*" by Arthur Sze first appeared in The *Virginia Quarterly Review* (Winter 2006). Reprinted by permission of the artist. All rights reserved.

"*Going Blind in April*" appears in Jeanne Shannon's book, *Angelus*, published in May 2006 by Fithian Press in McKinleyville, California. Reprinted by permission of the artist. All rights reserved.

"Slanted House" by Leslie Fox was previously published in *Earth's Daughters* 35th Anniversary Issue #69, *Signs.* Reprinted by permission of the artist. All rights reserved.

"*Many a Road*" by Jan Marie Baca previously appeared in *Corkscrew*, Volume 1, Issue 1. Descending Crane Press. Reprinted by permission of the artist. All rights reserved.

"*Late August*" by Lonnie Howard previously appeared in the *Santa Fe Literary Review*, 2006. Reprinted by permission of the artist. All rights reserved.

The editors would also like to acknowledge the support we received on this project from Merimee Moffitt, the members of NM Poetry Tangents, Carol Boss, Lisa Gill, KUNM radio in Albuquerque, Miriam Sagan and the Santa Fe Poetry Broadside, Dora McQuaid, the folks at www.southernnewmexico.com, the poetry and slam communities around New Mexico (especially that of the Albuquerque community), The ABQ Slam Council, NewMexico CultureNet, The English Department at the University of New Mexico, Kimberly Williams at San Juan College in Farmington, SOMOS in northern New Mexico, Dale Harris and Central Avenue magazine, as well as all of the newspapers, journals and television stations in the state who helped us to get the word out to our local talents , with a special thanks to the Mountain View Telegraph and KRQE-TV. We'd also like to extend a special thank you to the parents of our young writers, who allowed their inclusion in this book and continue to encourage their children to write and find expression. We deeply admire you for aiding the development of the next generation of poets!

Watering the Desert

Lately, I've taken to calling this state by the name which found itself on the cover of this anthology. Ironically, during a live television interview about the book, the very warm anchor-woman who interviewed me also referred to New Mexico as a modern mecca for poetry. While one might call this an unadulterated example of coincidence, I tend not to believe in luck; dumb or otherwise. It is funny how the universe leads us sometimes, and that tendency toward letting things happen organically has been an essential element in piecing together this anthology.

The actual point behind the preceding tangent is this; New Mexico....is a mecca of modern poetry. (Who didn't see that coming ...raise your hands?) If you were to cross-section the state like a sandwich, you would find a redolent vein of poetry ribboned throughout. While the obscure roast-beef metaphor is hunger induced, (lunch has come and gone. Even the typewriter is beginning to look rather edible), the truth is; New Mexico's valleys are verdant with enough *cuentos*, home-spun stories and poetry to feed any appetite. It is a voracious hunger for this poetry that laid the first step in the sand for us to begin this journey.

Over the last year and...several months, (I realize that's not very specific. My calendar's broken.) I have had the pleasure of working with Jessica Helen Lopez on numerous projects; founding NM Poetry Tangents, hosting and organizing events, building the state's largest website devoted to poetry, and hosting free monthly writing workshops, to name a few. All in all, I feel very positive about the things we have accomplished and I hope that we are contributing in some small way to the local arts. With that desire in place, it seemed a natural evolution to move forward by putting together a small compendium of the talents we have had the pleasure of reading, hearing and working with.

Although we were inspired by the number of amazing talents we knew existed here at home, we were still surprised by the overwhelming response we received to the open calls. We read over 1500 poems in all, and found poetry communities thriving in some very unexpected places. Even a number of ghost towns managed to whisper verse in our general direction! The experience was invigorating, to say the least. Personally, I was motivated to write a plethora of new pieces, and in the process I fell ever more in love with this weird, cathartic experience that is Southwest living. I hope you'll agree when you put the book down (somewhere after the third or fourth straight reading without sleep), that no one ever need go thirsty here. Language is a river, and as we let it rush over our tongues; we should do as the Tao suggests, and just go with it.

Our hope is that this collection will further illuminate the waters that feed this state, and carry the voices of her people home in the evenings. Many very accomplished poets call New Mexico home and we're exceedingly excited to have several of them within these pages. However, whether you're familiar with all (or any) of these poets yet or not, we are very proud to introduce you to some contemporary voices you may not yet have heard. When they're not reading and performing, many of these poets are working to build a broad community of activism as well (a fact evidenced by the biographies you can read in the back of the book). Aside from being home to the largest National Poetry Slam in history, and the 2005-2006 national champions, Albuquerque alone hosts five monthly slams and a variety of traditional readings and events. Working with children, ex-felons, the homeless, victims of trauma, and working towards political change and social awareness; you name it. If there's a cause worth fighting for, there's a New Mexican poet fighting. Whether page or stage, New Mexico is a poet's naughtiest, most Bohemian dreams come vividly alive.

Now, if you'll excuse me…it's snowing outside and that means it's time for me to strip down and go make anatomically correct snow angels in the yard. Either that or it's time for my medication. Either way, thank you for taking the time to wander through a tangent with me. Now, go feed your soul, and let us know how you like the book!

Contents

Ann Applegarth

She Would Have Flown a Hang-glider,
But Life Got In the Way

You'd expect it to appeal to a woman
who had flown in everything
from a Piper Cub to a 747,
a helicopter, hot air balloons,
and – with her kids – the Goodyear Blimp.

It looked effortless: strap on the frame,
trot to the edge of the cliff, and soar
like a condor (except more colorful) –
Icarus fulfilled in turquoise sky
above brown New Mexico desert.

Well, yes, sometimes the contraptions
fell. Crashed to earth with pilot's
dangling legs rigid in protest. But
she would wait until her youngest
grew up – just in case. On the day
he turned six, she vowed to fly on the
day he graduated from high school.

As six years went by, she nursed
her dream, watching others fly and land,
imagining lovely wind in her face,
wondering if she would feel weightless.
But then, the thing lovelier than flight
happened: another daughter born!
Instead of leaping from a cliff to fly,

she settled down to train her fledgling
and wait for that momentous flight.

And then? Well, then she had become
too old to fly, too faint of nerve, too
weak of knee. But sometimes, in the
summer, she would watch the gliders
soaring in the morning sun and wonder
why she ever thought that momentary
thrill could satisfy.

Tani Arness

In Your Bones

He said, *Bones.*
He said, *Bones, bones, bones, bones, rock.*
(It echoed that way in me.)
And I said, *Yes, yes* (like water).
He said, with finality (like ending summer),
Best thing that ever happened.
He spoke with the sounds of cranes in his throat.

His joins the voices flitting through me
now like phantoms,
haunting, arousing…
It is night. The sun has moved much further north.
I close my eyes and try to sleep,
but time has made creases in the sky
until it's impossible to see
the North Pole, the bending lights of God.

I hear my sister saying, *Well, yeah if you could do* that
[listen to your soul]
then you'd have all the answers. Then it'd be easy
I have not said to her, *Yes, that's why I do have all the*
answers. It is *easy.*
I do not want to argue.

Tani Arness

I believe in voices. I believe in
the traveling words of souls.
All I need is hours and quiet, shifting skies
moving the sun and moon.
Even science craves the listening.
We have put satellites into space now.
We have telephones now in places
where there are no roads or running water.
We want to know they're real, the voices, our souls.
I type a number into my phone;
the voice from my bones answers,

And suddenly everything, every place every person
 (their souls) exist at once.
He says he just left a meeting to discuss the misuse of
village "honey-bucket" receptacles.
He laughs and says,
It's like we're still living in the dark ages here, huh?
I answer, *No, it's like you still have the light*
before the darkness.

Casa Mechicah

Yo! – Cantiflas!
Who discovered Amerika?

Nobody.

We never reported it missing.
Until the violence
was visited, heaped upon us.

We have always been here.
On the back of a crocodile,
in the heart of Quetzalcoatl.

As eagles and jaguars.
As chief speakers.
As Tlacaellel.

Lady and lord
of the Mexica house.
Co-rulers
of the internal
and the external.

Jan Marie Baca

Many a Road

I dreamt you were dead, Stephen.
Your friends sat in wigs,
high heels and make-up
around your open grave
smoking cigarettes,
talking in low, smiling voices
about your perfect teeth.

Pennsylvania autumn, 1989,
on the steps of the hospital, waiting,
walking up and down with your hands
stuffed in your pockets.
the test results came back
negative. You would live
for now.

In the winter we sat
in your mother's basement.
Pencils, paints, a bottle of Burgundy.
We listened to our tunes like we could back then
and you tried to kiss me,
Stephen. Your face so serious
and tender, I had to laugh.
I already knew you didn't want me that way.
You couldn't.

Jan Marie Baca

In summer, we planned the rest of our lives.
The move to New Orleans,
the best-selling novels, the boat-
we would sail everywhere,
be decadent…
Disappear.

So many years later, I saw you
in my apartment with the broken windows, the
holes in the walls.
I hardly knew you.
And, true to plan,
you did disappear.

Did you make it to New Orleans, Stephen?
Or did the coke and the queens
drag you down, used, wasted,
to some obscure hole
in the ground? I refuse
that vision and choose you on the boat,
a million-five in the bank, sun
glinting off of your impossible white teeth.

Ray Michael Baca

Where have I been, you ask?

I'm down in the way cool desert, living amongst the
roadrunners and coyotes, and dodging giant tumbleweeds,
and watching the sky all day long, and listening to the Rio
Grande flow by even when I'm sleeping, and especially
when I'm dreaming, with a warm heart and cool hands
these days, here in the heat of this cold, cold summer, even
when I'm with someone and enjoying a few more drinks
than I really need, and being lonely even when I'm with
one of those nameless, pretty people who I can see as
insincere, whose faces suddenly change to send an
ominous chill through me when they don't think I'm
looking, and missing someone all the while who probably
wasn't right for me anyway, but only, of course, when I'm
most vulnerable like first thing in the morning when the
doves at the window attempt to awaken me, and last thing
at night when I stare at the nuanced shadows of my
darkness, but there are breaking clouds on the horizon,
hopefully ones that are more than just metaphors, …

Jimmy Santiago Baca

Matanza to Welcome Spring

For Pat and Victorio

Spread eagle sheep legs wide,
wire hooves to shed beams,
and sink blade in neck wool,
'til the gray eyes drain of life
like cold pure water
from a tin pail.

> (It kicked, choking on nasal blood,
> liquid gasping coughs
> spattered blood over me.)

Slit down belly, scalp rug wool
skin away, pinch wool back
with blade to pink flesh, ssst ssst ssst
inch by inch, then I sling
whole carcass in bloody spray over fence.

> (Close to its face, I swear
> it gift-heaved a last breath
> from its soft black nose
> and warmed my nostril hairs
> as I sniffed the dark smell
> of its death.)

Mesquite in hole
boils water in the iron cauldron

which steam-cooks

hind quarter

on grill across cauldron.

       Tonight I invite men and women

       con duende,

       who take a night in life

       and forge it into iron

       in the fire of their vision.

Aragon has gone

to the river to play his drum.

I hear the deep pom pom pom.

Round bonfire

Alicia squats, ruffles sheaf of poems,

while Alejandro tunes guitar.

Shadows dance round

stones that edge the fire.

       (In Alejandro's boot

       a knife hilt glimmers.)

Their teeth gleam grease juice

       (as do those of the children, who play

       in the dark behind us).

There is fear

in the horse's eye

corralled nearby.

Jimmy Santiago Baca

(Hear the drum on the Rio Grande.

Boom pom boom pom....)

Blood sizzles,

moist alfalfa in the air,

bats flit above the flames.

I toss a gleaming bone to spirits

in the orchard,

and Gonzales yells,

with his old earthen voice,

"Play, *hombre, Canta, mujer*! Sing!

Sing the way the old ones sang!"

Tonight life is

lust

death

hunger

violence

innocence

sweetness

honor

hard work

and tomorrow I will go

to church.

But tonight

I leap into

37

impulse, instinct,

into the burning

of

     this moment.

     (I commit myself! One moment to the next

     I am chasm jumper and silence is

      a blue fire on my papery soul. I construct

     out of nothing. I am air, am labyrinth,

     place with no entry or exit,

     am a smoking mirror.

     Commit myself! Storms stroke my heart

     and destroy its neat furrows.

     My words are mule teams,

     that loosen, pound, hurl, out and up,

     and leave me standing in the open, naked,

     with star flame roar, life opening….

     Commit myself!)

Hear the two hands

bleed along the river beating

drumskins,

deep sounds of thu-uba,

of magic, despair, joy,

     emotions trance-weave through sound,

Jimmy Santiago Baca

thumba, thumba, thumba.

Follow drum,
    thumba thumba thumba,
    umba umba umba
    ba-ba ba-ba
    thumba thumba thumba,
hear hearts mate with earth
in song,
spiral toward death
      in its long thuuumba,
toward life again
    in ba-ba-ba-ba.

The sound is stain on purity,
is cry of broken thing,
drum does not wither beneath bed,
but rises heart
    into newness around us,
all around us,
    come follow   Follow the drum,
    thumba thumba thumba
            ba-ba-ba
    thumba thumba thumba
            ba-ba-ba,

            of living!

David Baker

"Ode to Jorge Luis Borges"

I read poetry last night.

Stuccoed homes in cinnamon shadows.

Soft murmurs of a river flowing.

Oranges dropping wet, full, ripe.

Death creeping with each breath.

El Recolleto cemetery fading in mists.

Stars float above BBQ smoke.

Bolivar's hoof beats echo across alley ways.

I read great poetry last night.

Weeping, with each image.

Afraid of my failings.

Yearning to be better than I am.

Multicolored roofs,

line streets of South American bohemia.

Evita's ghostly hand reaches from dirty walls.

Football fans cheer modern day gladiators.

While the hour of the dove finds its rest.

I read fantastic poetry last night.

I read till my eyes could not see white from black.

I read till my dead

perched in tree branches outside my door.

Listening to my thoughts,

my heart as they longed for more.

I read a poets work last night and I am better for it.

David Baker

Poorer am I, for I feel my worth fade with each exhalation.

My lips parted, my tongue coated

 those parched instruments.

I let go of my fears, and was

transported through portals of space.

Where my anxiety was matched

by the grand paseo of the universe.

I read, and I read.

I read till I was reading in my sleep.

In a one bedroom shack,

in the middle of the desert, on a dead end street.

Hakim Bellamy

Agony and Endurance

Pepper me with pepper spray.

Shower me with acid rain.

Feed me nails so I can up-chuck articulate constructs
        that remedy all your ill fortunes.

Witch-doctor of words
has a pretty good idea of which words spell spells.

Batter me with batteries…
so my bruises charge me to write lessons
        taken from wounds,
so when I look back and laugh at how things
wound up
        once I was not so wound up,
but removed from the punishment…

I still remember why.

A constant reminder like black eyes
        when you have to face the face
            someone else got sick of.

Taper me with tape…
so I stay as tightly groomed as a groom and appear
        just as polished,

gagged like a good kidnapping when I carelessly utter
criticisms that steal the youthful
    enthusiasm of another's great ideas.

Cloud me with tear gas…
        so I don't forget to weep when I count cottontails
        in New Mexico sky,
        while those in industrial ghettos of Newark
            may never see enough stars to run
                out of fingers to count.

Count like they do in schools,
        but not in the electoral colleges,

like statistics they are doomed to be a part of.
        Never old enough to take courses in it
          and learn their contributions.

So illuminate me with moonlight
        when the stars that burned out light-years ago
          stop pretending they're still there,

and the sun stops rotating because it's scared of
       repeating history.

We stop revolving because going in circles is
       about as thrilling as re-reading a mystery.

And the insanity stops.
       Gravity loses its weight.

I fill in the holes in spotless minds and…

drink at funerals
       and weddings;
after all, both are family reunions.

I eat at child-birth because I am hungry for life…

And in my last days…
       my hunger wanes, like the living daylights
         like daytime
           like days
             like time.

Like I'm tired of torturing myself.

Hakim Bellamy

Tired of trying to be something I'm not.

Like strong.

Like normal.

Like   perfect.

Like   myself.

Like   Alive.

Leslie Bentley

Penmanship

Old man's hands.
An old fountain pen.
Old man is trying to make "a"
have just the right curve.

Penmanship:
Pen.   Man.   Ship.
Dry, shaky, resentful.
Must get it right.

Grandson sits with his Italian nose in a book.
Not metaphorically,
but he really cannot look up
to reveal the slap on his face.

Grandfather gives that look;
his inky fingers smearing the alphabet.
Boy pretends to read
but he has a dream behind his eyes:

an African landscape
floats inside his chest

(it is hotter and more colorful
the closer you get to the equator).

Boy is adventurous young man
leading his favorite ox,
singing warrior songs into the beaded breast of
his beloved;
a woman with skin the color of deep adobe desert.

Old man fumbles with paper.
Grimy walking stick.
Dry lips.
The inkwell is empty.

For the boy
it's a time for sore eyes—
stinging from dreaming too much;
writes "Africa" in perfect letters.

Ben Bormann

Pekoe

I saw tendrils of blood

       reaching out of my brewing teabag

       in the pale fluorescent light

       of indoor echo electricity.

Expanding in my tea as Waits belted out odes

       to his 1974 Saturday nights,

       hearts and ghosts playing down

       like midnight sky's diamonds on his windshield.

Flowing into my tea

       like dreams where you swim in the sky

       and see yourself

       through everyone's eyes.

Blood in billowing fluid clouds,

       seeping into my incarnation of

       what the Zen masters claimed

       was necessary to see the world's truth,

Tea, the liquid of lavish life.

And there was blood in mine,

       bold arms hugging the water,

       squeezing transparency from the cup.

But it still turned that bright brown

       that any decent orange

       and black cut pekoe should,

though I'm thinking this time

it's the blood oxidizing,

like the ugly mud color it turns

when it stains your favorite shirt

after a border skirmish

with your lover's new man.

This blood in my tea,

it was a water-based augury,

and I became a witch reading the future

in its deceitful sweetness.

Reading words yet written.

Seeing creations yet fathomed.

Living the lives of those unborn.

My tea's mixture with life's elixir

smelled rich and familiar

and with every sip

I taste reminiscence.

And I realized it was mine,

it somehow snuck into the silk pouch

and sheltered itself,

waiting for the chemical exodus

induced by the boiling water.

Waiting like a lynx,

a feline spring of pound-for-pound energy

equivalent to an atom bomb of awakening

as it pounced and was pulled

through the air

toward its prey,

me.

My own blood twisting vision,

tingling taste buds and traveling

past light speed to my brain,

giving me glimpses of my life to come,

glancing my dancing children

in my unfocused peripherals.

The words the future holds

in its open-page palm are mine,

The inventions are new systems

replacing the rusted steel structures

forming the unstable base

I now live on.

The lives are my children.

And the blood in my tea

dissipated and evaporated,

went to rejoin the capillaries

of my future family.

Leaving a mild iron taste

as I drank the last bit of it down.

Coming in From Yesterday

Intact, my wounded heart.
Sore, patches bare.
Love lost
give credence to miracles
that yesterday has gone,
leaving nothing in its wake
save breath in quick gasps,
Stung by realizations of
how dark the night can be!

I wept upon your pillow,
a beggar
pleading for the morrow
to come and melt my sorrow.

Deliver me God of light.
Carry me into a new day.
Lift the veil, nocturnal, leaving
nothing but a memory
of coming in from yesterday.

Debbi Brody

From China to Chimayo

Transformation, a divine habit
in the bottom drawer.

Pop out pill packs, hard
cellophane, forgiving aluminum.

Chalky white potion boxed in red and white.
A needle, your eye in mind, your vein,

not a dropper. A spindle, naked,
no one spins anymore. Clothes

from China, cheaper, from
were opium used to come.

Now it's everywhere. Black
tar heroin in Chimayo – up

from Mexico. A whole new lexicon
of secret deaths, unpolished turquoise,

obsidian on the back seat of a burnt out
Bel Air. Chamisa grows through rusted

Debbi Brody

floor boards, rice grass and mold,
best friends in the shredded back seat.

Addiction howls like salt
on pulsating wounds.

Lying in alfalfa, sand dusted
shoulders, the dead

under ribboned tires, cracked
by summer's dry heaves.

Maestro Teacher

Voice

    Give them voice.

    Child's song, poetry.

    Value their pearls.

Read, Regurgitate.

Read, Question.

Read, Write.

Write, Voice.

Rights,

Voiced.

Poetas have been Politically persecuted

    By the powering factions

Because we dare have voice.

Many martyrs leave their voice

    Floating, dancing

    From pen to paper.

      Script.

Whispering caresses of love,

Shouting orgasmic lust,

Spouting political rhetoric

    Of ones soul.

Maestro teaching voice.

Amendments,

Silenced,

Contoured,

Masked,

Ridiculed.

Waves of poetas speak.

    Shout out

With ink and pen.

We need no more Martyred sons.

Ancient shores claim far too many.

Warring acts of destruction.

    Always leaving fathers asking

    For children to be brought home.

        Voice

        Spoken

        Voice

        Heard

        Speak.

Ioanna Carlsen

Eighteenth Century Japanese Screen

Sometimes, later in the evening,
I think I see the figures move.

Little people, walking
through the dirt streets of a village
dressed in black or light blue,

leading an occasional white horse;

the town,
dressed in the light of the passed, wearing another
dimension.

...

A lake inhabits the second panel.

A town the first,
a park the third.
I cannot see the fourth.

It is hidden by a wall of the present.

Occasional though they are,
why are all the horses white you might ask:
string theory I answer –

with eleven more dimensions

the unusual could be normal,
the normal stranger---
The peaked roofs of the houses,

the globular trees, imperfect lakes,
the temples like mountains,
could be one bridge after another,

leading out of this world.

      ...

Everything here is imaginary,
or dead – the planes inside the picture
could contain both,

while pretending to be neither-

Cranes, swans and egrets,
origami designs in the landscape,

Ioanna Carlsen

which appear to be
perpetually getting away
in the gold, gilded background
that must be autumn.

We live only in one dimension-

Such is luck, human,
to look at a picture and hear sadness
cry like a duck flying over a lake

that has fallen asleep
in a twilight that visits forever.

I Saw Peru

I saw Peru, a closed eyelid,
from Lima to Cuzco,
on a train ride, parched
as dried grass.
Skinny spotted cows,
sterile chickens,
dirty children ran, ran
to catch a piece of fruit
thrown by a tourist
from the train
going fast, past them forever.

Thousands of grubby potatoes at the market
and barefoot Incan descendants
with derbies and broad-rimmed bonnets –
I saw. Cobalt blue colors, sunflower yellow dyes
and bright spices,
wrapped in a bit of brown paper
for a small price.
Everyone toothless and shy.

Ana Castillo

I heard Bolivian tunes throughout
over the airwaves and live,
sung by the blind for a few s*oles*,
sung for a hope.

And dust everywhere,
along the banisters in cathedrals and museums,
in the president's palace. The entire plumbing system
backed up to Chile, out to Colombia,
so that the very young
and very old pee in broad daylight.
Beaches of Lima strewn with glass and garbage.
Cabdrivers warn tourists—don't stay out too late.

Let the eat *choclo*! Someone seems to have declared,
and a small piece of fried trout on special days.
They may have instant coffee but not ask for milk.
The starved cows in the field have none to give.
No one has much to give but a smile
with a "Please, *mamita linda*, won't you buy
a freshly made tamal? No meat, of course,
just cornmeal…c'mon, don't be mean"

-1998, Chicago

Inara Cedrins

Green Moon

Last night I dreamed of you who will not go away,
de fina, you who were cruel to me. A stolen cactus
the size of a dinner-plate set low against my patio wall,
I'm nestled here like in Chaco Canyon,
with community, while you
think I'm still halfway around the world. In the dream
I'd brought two men with me
to the clearing where you lived,
telling them you were important to me. You ignored us
but knew I was there, indulgent,
like the time you told me to wait
and delayed for hours, clinking about in
the darkroom with silver canisters.
We dipped into the stream with bright tin cans,
the light on my face
dazzling as my new environment; the only plant I know
the name of here, yellow *chamiso*. So we enter the last
quarter of our lives, *de fina*, poison spent:
I was dragging an immense shrub
through the house at the end,
and as we left I said, *I know you love me.*
I live in the place that is my last dream
niched, walls of soft sand,
cactus like a green moon that will rise.

Sandra Cisneros

Down There

> At that moment, Little Flower scratched herself
> where one never scratches oneself.
> from "The Smallest Woman in the World"
>> – Clarice Lispector

Your poem thinks it's *bad*.
Because it farts in the bath.
Cracks its knuckles in class.
Grabs its ball is public
and adjusts—one,
then the other—
back and forth like Slinky. No,
more like the motion
of a lava lamp.
You follow me?

Your poem thinks it
cool to pee in the pool.
Waits for the moment
someone's watching before
it sticks a finger up
its nose and licks
it. Your poem's weird.

Sandra Cisneros

The kind that swaggers in like Wayne
or struts its stuff like Rambo.
The kind that learned
to spit at 13 and still
is doing it.

It blames its bad habits
on the Catholic school.
Picked up words that
snapped like bra straps.
Learned words that ignite
on their own gas
like a butt hole flower.
Fell in love with words
that thudded like stones and sticks.
Or stung like fists.
Or stank like shit
gorillas throw at zoos.

Your poem never washes
its hands after using the can.
Stands around rolling
toilet paper into wet balls
it can toss up to the ceiling
just to watch them stick.
Yuk. Yuk.

Sandra Cisneros

Your poem is a used rubber
sticky on the floor
the next morning,

the black elephant
skin of the testicles,
hairy as kiwi fruit
and silly,
the shaving
stubble against the purity
of porcelain,

one black pubic
hair on the sexy
lip of toilet seat,

the swirl of spit
with a cream of celery
center,

a cigarette
stub sent hissing
to the piss pot,

half-finished
bottles of beer reeking

their yeast incense,

the miscellany of maleness:

nail clippers and keys,

tobacco and ashes,

pennies quarters nickels dimes and

dollars folded into complicated origami,

stub of ticket and pencil and cigarette, and

the crumb of the pockets

all scattered on the Irish

linen of the bedside table.

Oh my little booger,

it's true.

Because someone once

said Don't

do that!

you like to do it.

Baby, I'd like to mention

the Tampax you pulled with your teeth

once in a Playboy poem*

and found it, darling, not so bloody.

Not so bloody at all, in fact.

Hardly blood cousin

* John Updike's "Cunts" in Playboy. (January 1984), 163

except for an unfortunate
association of color
that makes you want to swoon.

Yes,
I want to talk at length about Men-
struation. Or my period.
Or the rag as you so lovingly put it.
All right then.

I'd like to mention my rag time.

Gelatinous. Steamy
and lovely to the light to look at
like a good glass of burgundy. Suddenly
I'm artist each month.
The star inside this like a ruby.
Fascinating bits of sticky
I-don't-know-what-stuff.

The afterbirth without the birth.
The gobs of a strawberry jam.
Membrane stretchy like
saliva in your hand.

It's important you feel its slickness,
understand the texture isn't bloody at all.
That you don't gush
between the legs. Rather,
it unravels itself like string
from some deep deep center—
like a Russian subatomic submarine,
or better, like a mad Karlov cackling
behind beakers and blooping spirals.
Still with me?

Oh I know, darling,
I'm indulging, but indulge
me if you please.
I find the subject charming.

In fact,
I'd like to dab my fingers
in my inkwell
and write a poem across the wall.
"A Poem of Womanhood"
Now wouldn't that be something?

Sandra Cisneros

Words writ in blood. But no,
not blood at all, I told you.
If blood is thicker than water, then
menstruation is thicker than brother-
hood. And the way

it metamorphosizes! Dazzles.
Changing daily
like starlight.
From the first
transparent drop of light
to the fifth day chocolate paste.

I haven't mentioned smell. Think
Persian rug.
But thicker. Think
cello.
But richer.
A sweet exotic snuff
from an ancient prehistoric center.
Dark, distinct,
and excellently
female.

Kathleen Clute

Smoke Signals

I've decided not to write a poem for you.
You let me down.
I wanted you to fight & live & cackle at me
when I turned 100.
You wanted marriage more than anything else in life,
and look what it cost you:
I throw you out of my house
before you're dead even 24 hours.
Later you come back—I turn my heart away,
and the next few weeks I am full of strange denials—
I won't play Chopin for you—
I won't give you a requiem—
I won't admit that I thirst for the mischief
that arrived at my door dancing in your wild violet eyes.
I am stubbornly serene.
I will endure, even without mischief.

But you are better at haunting me than I am
at resisting you.
We continue our earthly lunches at the celestial cafe.
A tardy ghost, you're late for your own hauntings,
but you arrive mirthful,
brimming with the secrets I need to learn
to attain ecstasy,

and you are so glorious I believe you.
Against my wishes, I lose your wisdom as I wake up.

Like the day you sat in my car,
laughing over the one thing I needed to understand
to drop all pretense and be perfect,
while we flew down a dusty road:
you may be telling the truth but I can't hear it.
Nor did you hear the truth I shouted back at you.
We are matched in that as in all other ways—
noon and midnight eternally linked,
the opposite faces of the sun.

You haunted me until I surrendered.
I've sent you a Valentine the way you taught me—
through the fireplace,
kissed with flame and smoke.

I had to do it, you were shrieking so loudly
at the card shop—
every Valentine belonged to you, only you—
you, my gypsy self, my sister love,
you who tell me the truths I will not hear
and never let me down.

One I–love–you cannot compass us,
so I send you two
and finally the visitations stop.

I could do anything for you except be a man.
I have bought you a ring.
I'm wearing it on my left hand,
next to the marriage finger.

You trust me again
and I have forgiven you for dying.
I know you'll cackle when I turn 100.
The front door is open—
come visit anytime.

Huey, David and Bobby

Huey P. Newton,
along with
Bobby Seale and
David Hilliard,
chose to create
revolution as an option.
Vietnam prompted white and black mouths
to beautifully define gray areas, screaming,
"Free Huey".
And they did.

Out for others' blood to spill,
cracked from inner halves of
strange fruit.
They wanted to squeeze Angela dry
but didn't have a leg to stand on, for
the gun's drawn.

A struggle withdrawn
because federal gun play intimidated innocent people.

They stood in
defense,
not aggression,

because
government action put
I have a dream speeches
to rest, like it was backwards day
and there was no time for more
nightmares.

WE WANT FREEDOM
WE WANT DECENT HOUSING
WE WANT DECENT EDUCATION
AND
AN IMMEDIATE END TO ALL WARS OF
AGGRESSION.

This country persecuted a people tired
of saying
please and no!
So,
trained to take things
they decided to roll
the dice and pay with lives
because
time lost was that valuable,
equal rights that important,
and the color of one's skin,
although not a choice,

had manifested itself into a responsibility
that one could not deny.

Poised and determined to stand by their cause,
David, Bobby and Huey
were ready to die.
Birthing children who understood a struggle
like a painful second language.
I promise we shall revisit a time
where fists meant more than
fighting,
and where there is more to fight over
than corners or boroughs.
We are at a tipping point,
black and brown people melting
above the pot and refusing
to flow passively into
Assimilated American History.
This is His-Story.
The superior capitalist
American
Idealist.
Ours is yet to be written.

Will it require blood?
Those on the outside looking in
can decide what the death toll needs to be.

We are sacrificing our children
to everyday life.
At least in battle they'll die
decently.

The fight for rights may no longer
allow for civil interplay.
Amerikka is birthing a
Revolutionary bastard.

He's aware of his unapparent history.
And he's here to
Tell his story,
But first…
He sits silently.
Rifle in hand, heart in throat,
A struggle waiting.

Dr. Wayne Crawford

Night Moves in the Desert

Mexican Elders stoop
in the light outside
our bedroom window
and listen to our ceiling fan
swirl, usually on low, perhaps
believing both the sun
and wind come here
to slow down and cool off.

When we blow out our
candles, branches incline
toward the desert moon
above Picacho Peak.

Now and then, for pleasure,
leaves rustle.

Jasmine Cuffee

A Blessing

There's this angel
learning to play the piano across the street from me
and through these hard walls and half open doors adjacent
from one another
I'm eavesdropping on creation.

Half-listening.
This angel, she's playing one note;
One note, not exactly strumming my pain,
but has me believing in something.

Now I don't know what keys she's tapping,
whether black or white;
A or G or both at the same time,

but these four chambers, they're rattling.
She's ripping out my heart and eating from it.
She's playing my song, all seven salty seas of it,

and I can't help but wonder how
she knows me so well;
 how she can trace every vein like rosary beads
and paint my blood heaven.

Jasmine Cuffee

She's inspiring me to be holy so I gather
shattered glass shards;
the H Aesop stole from heritage
the pens I stole from Wal-greens
and the first line from every
Langston Hughes poem I've ever read

and purged myself Godly

She's got me praying for flight ya'll.
Eating sacramental words and drinking lots of wine.

She's playing one note;
one note, not exactly strumming my pain
but has me believing in something.

Messenger

(to Naomi who chose ten months *in utero*)

Upside down on mesh,
the full brown fur-fist hangs.
Jittery and thralled, I draw close,
examine the panting velvet - its fine pinched nose,
red web veining each translucent ear.

Scraped off the screen door,
the bat falls ajump with panicked wings
to my Folgers Coffee tin.
I carry it to the pin oak's lowest fork,
slide the creature from metalline sides.

Bellows of skin work air
like a kite's rattle,
a fanned labor.
as it flaps across the street,
sticks only seconds on a house gable and turns

to face me with the face
of a child,
and sails back toward me.

Janet Eigner

The air swarms, gray, viscous
as I turn and run for home.

This is not human time.
Only children, they say, hear the bat's pitch
but I'm caught in a net,
my shriek as silent as the bat's.
I slam my front door, watch it

hunch on the next house's brick.
All day we peer out at each other,
more alike than not.
Feel the blood message.
Recall the hieroglyphs written across my womb

    say Safety,
    say Welcome

by the child
suspended head
down.

Damien Flores

City Built of Ghosts

Where the sidewalk breaks
in the crumble of downtown,
the cement bows
into a grin of footsteps.

Where dirt and wind-torn branches
gather like strings of a requiem
composed of the city's fingers
outstretched and gnarled
from the fury of concrete.

Beneath the solace of asphalt
there is a temple rising like a slow moon
beneath the street,
beneath their gospel,
in the bellowing of Nahuatl prayers.

In the grinding altar of mumble
through mid-day traffic.

And the sidewalk breaks more with each step
as its gray smile
flashes toothless and guilty.

Damien Flores

Toothless and guilty
like us who step over the cracks
to dodge the city's ghosts
at our feet
and think of nothing
as our distractions shout our names.

As we walk the dragging pilgrimage
work in the morning,
the bank at noon,
the bars at night.

Cities were built with a purpose,
like we were built with a purpose
and are forgotten
like our streets that collapse
under the weight
of our days.

Leslie A. Fox

Slanted House

The Virgin of Guadalupe sits in a small box on my dashboard. She looks serene with pretty little flames dancing around her in the lime green glow from the console. She stands on a crescent moon and she prays for me; sending up prayers of supplication. The smoke from the cigarettes that I puff is a prayer wafting from my fingers like incense, out of my mouth and nostrils, swirling around the Virgin and out the window into the night as I drive away from New Orleans.

I pray because I need to stay awake. I have been driving too long and am beginning to see things. I saw a Skinwalker a ways back, running along beside my truck before I crossed the Louisiana border. I thought the walking dead were only seen in the Southwest. But what do you expect in a state where they bury the dead above ground. I saw him from the corner of my eye. I looked and he was gone, but at one point he jumped in front of me for a moment; up ahead on the road, hopped into the center of the highway as if playing a game of chicken, then vanishing. I don't know who I am praying to since I don't believe in God anymore. I pray to the Virgin of Guadalupe because she is a woman and because she's really an Aztec goddess dressed in Catholic clothes.

Jobs in New Orleans are transient with the ebb

and flow of tourists. My job at the Daiquiri Shack started with Mardi Gras, ended with the Jazz Festival and the receding tide of happy revelers. I am glad to be fleeing New Orleans. Houses sink there. When I rode in the taxi with Ivy she warned me before we arrived that her house was slanted.

"Slanted?"

"It tilts at an angle, you know, it's sinking on one side," she explained. "It can be a little unsettling when you first walk in, but you get used to it."

Then her hand fell on my knee and I forgot about the slanted house. When I walked in the front door, I felt a little dizzy as if I were about to fall over. I thought it was just because I was drunk and it wasn't until morning that I realized the house was, in fact, slanted. Walking through the hall, I had to compensate for the tilt by leaning over a little. She served me coffee and toast in an awkward silence. Had we made love? I was too embarrassed to ask. I sipped my coffee with chicory. I had to hold myself back from rolling one of the oranges from the bowl across the table. She left the room to answer the phone. Her kitchen chairs had wheels on them and I pushed off and rolled down the linoleum floor, just making it back to my side of the table by the time she returned.

It has something to do with the water table, with

building a city on top of a swamp. I began to notice other houses, buildings, leaning this way and that all in a delightful state of decay. One house that I saw was bending in the middle, snapped in two, both ends of the house sticking up higher as if it had sprouted wings and was getting set to fly away, out of that moldy place—fly west to the desert and dry out. There are no boundaries in that town, where the dead are buried above ground because the alternative is too morbid. The earth cannot hold them. No boundaries between the world below and that on top. The dead rising to the surface and the living sinking down to meet them.

I pray to the Virgin even though I was never a Catholic. I was Protestant and learned that Catholics were pagans because they had all of those saints and they pray to Mary. I guess that makes me a pagan now. I do not worry who she sends the prayers to, I just pray. I haven't seen anyone running alongside my truck in a while, so I assume it's working. When I get to the next town, I will pull into a well-lighted convenience store and lie down on my bench-seat for a few minutes. Just close my eyes for a little while. I need to close my eyes. I wonder if the Skinwalker was just trying to keep me from falling asleep at the wheel and running off the road. I appreciate the help, but I will be just as glad if I never see him again.

Beginnings

I am

a grand adventure

I am the final frontier

I am the far off plains

the rush of dark woods

the headwaters of the dreamtime

I am Blue Mountain and Old Village

I am the fields in winter

I am the orchards in spring

I am the arroyo

and the banks of the Rio Grande

I am the mesa at sunrise

I am the Sandias at dusk

I am the cracks in the asphalt

the weeds in the concrete

I am the stone wall

the chain-link fence

the interstate

I am the blood of the earth

I am a restless heart

I am

a grand adventure

I am

the beginning

Brief Encounter

She gives him her bowl of tears.
He drinks to soothe his thirst.
Dry-eyed, her tears fade in his flesh.
Compassion's subtle ring rubs his skin,
causes humble lyrics to roll off his tongue.
A brown goddess dances around
his dirty shoe laces,
her skirt slapping his legs.
Yellow uneven teeth spread-eagled
in front of her halo.
The kingdom of birds
leads its army across the sky
to the beat   the beat of his words.
They flap in unison,
saluting the compassionate woman,
the humble man.

Lisa Gill

Allumette

I saw you walk the street drunk with doubt.
Your posture was a prophet I have words with.
It was Corpus Christi and you'd eaten so much god
your head rolled about and then dropped —plunk—
into your hands. Some days a person can catch a swoon
as easily as a book of matches tossed casually.
When I heard you call out, "allumette," I got hot
as a girl should struck by a single French word
on an American street. Moreover, since I'm always
searching for a light I knew what you meant.
Nonetheless I had a head full of unpolished cutlery
 and could only point to another woman wearing sandals
and suggest maybe she could help you. And then walk on.

You followed
blindly
as if I was dancing
and my feet weren't dirty.

You followed
wanting
as if my mouth were
a whole hive of honey
my body nothing

but wild thistle
being pollinated.

You followed
plagued
as if my nipples were locusts
and you believed
that only such finely veined wings
could free your head
from the cage
of your wracking
fingers.

Later you'd tell me that all you know about sex
you learned from Jane Austin and we'd laugh.
You and I want there to be a good book
for everything. Now you want to be a priest.
I am more practical. I want to be dirt
in an alfalfa field. I want to be flooded
with ditch water so ducks swim
my belly. I want to be so soft
that migrating birds coo
nestle down and leave tracks, scar me
with hard-toed lines.
I expect the inevitable drought
and then
I want the wind.

Lisa Gill

So perhaps we do have matching sadnesses,

some small place filled with a long ache, or a bad tooth.

These days your lips part for god and foreign languages

but I haven't even been to a dentist in years.

Last opened my mouth to gasp at something you said

that night we got drunk on silly tales of

19th century authors,

my dog, your saints, things we saw in movies or in visions.

I told you mine, spilled it, lost it into your ears,

pronouncing the words like another girl's Hail Mary.

When I stopped you popped the question and I gasped.

Sometimes a girl waits centuries to hear one quick

turn of phrase. You said four words: Will you marry

God? So today I am Salome and you are John.

I wanted this, your head resting on my lap

with your body elsewhere, tucked back in some quiet

bed at the monastery. You only look at me out of habit.

Out of habit, I run my hands through your hair,

put all my fingers on your face, on your lips,

into your small mouth, pushing your bitten teeth

apart, so I—who am I to experience ecstasy—can touch

my fingers to your tongue. Inhale and ask me again.

This time you have the right words. Tomorrow

Lisa Gill

I may be a tattoo artist inking images of Mary
inside my own thighs for practice, perhaps
yesterday we both lost our heads but for now
I've put all the sharp objects away because
I want to be the woman the priest you intend to be saw:
not so uncouth, perhaps called,
smitten with something holy.

You honestly thought I could be a nun. You were right
and I could kiss you and you were wrong
and I will miss you
when it works out that once again
I stay in this world
while you go to god.

Gary Glazner

The Art of War

We, each of us, keep what we remember in our hearts.
We, all of us, keep what we remember in museums.
In this way, museums beat inside us.

- from Museum Heart by Alberto Rios

Here is a list of things that are missing:
The Lyre of Ur with its strings

made of hummingbird tongues
& umbilical cords of the newly dead.
Rivers are missing and all the songs that rivers sing.
The marble statue of Eros.
For is he not love in all its manifestations?
Does not love tremble for the death of tyrants?
Is not love's fragile arrow among the missing?
The ivory lion attacking a Nubian.
So even hunger is missing.
The Abu Ghurayb prisoners are missing,
although you can find some carving dead songs in the soil,
the river-less hymns that those buried alive must sing.
Some singing songs of freedom in the limitless air,
happy to be free of death's slick black noose.
The marble statue of Poseidon is missing.
So which of our Gods shall we give the sea?
How quickly we divvy up the spoils of war.

Gary Glazner

The scrolls of the earliest known writing appear

to have been destroyed by fire.

They are not missing we must learn to read ashes and the

bones of ashes.

The water works, the hospitals, the schools, and the

highways all are missing.

Let the looted art be loved.

Let the burned books be light.

Let history judge us by the things we do not save.

Yesterday I walked through a park

dedicated to the preservation of Petroglyphs.

Strike a boulder directly with a hammerstone

to remove the dark, desert varnish.

The image closest to the trail was of two birds

joined at the waist,

a concentric spiral and a star.

I am lucky they reveal themselves at all.

All living things dance in a never-ending circle

made of stars.

Can you smell the desert air?

Would I give up that smell

for the perfect never ending poem?

Would I die for you?

Is that the art of war?

Grace

Some Day Her Prince Will Come

Some day her prince will come.....

she...had a baby...for him...

every morning without fail
she lives in the shadows of ol' wives tales
of how her prince charming will come just to save her
and want to give to her all of his favor

and how he on bended knee
will profess his love for all eternity
and to him
she will reveal her innermost soul
and give over to him
her nubile body
whole

she...had a baby..for him...

she knew him only for a brief time
he spoke to her in words as fine as wine
intoxicating her young and fertile mind

Grace

he entered her life
with style and ease
no father to teach her
of men who could reach her
at that special place hidden between her knees

he stroked her mind
with great expectations
he kissed her lips
just on the tips

as he envisioned her virginity
that he would rip from her child-like body
so sweet and wanting

she remembers the day she became a woman
cause it is still haunting her
day
and night

as she looks disgustedly
at herself in the mirror
her body has changed
her life re-arranged and how
it all happened has become

Grace

painfully
clearer

she...had a baby...for him...

she remembers how sweet he was to her

he comforted her
he complimented her
he pursued until her desire did stir

no daddy to guide her or lead her away
from these type of men
who only see her as prey
and fill her mind
with dreams of perfection
and tempt her heart with promised connections
when it's only a game
to satisfy his erection
of a world without fathers
who give their protection

so she laid down with him
he said he did love her

Grace

so she allowed him to enter
under her Barbie doll covers

he came in the night
in the full moon light
and her mother?
like the others
didn't know of the luster and did really trust her

to be home alone
she had a cell phone
but he was determined to plant his seed in her womb

she...had a baby...for him...

now the fated fairy tale's over
but still she dreams on
and nobody notices the cuts on her arm

she changes the diapers
lost track of school
she takes special meds that change the color of her stool
and every other day
her mother calls her a fool
and demands that she get down on her knees and pray

Grace

'cause now
she's thrown her very life away
just like her mom
and nobody notices the cuts on her arm

as her friends have become razor blades and safety pins
and her young life now
is turned outside in
and daily
she's reminded of her one visible sin

at 14/she's HIV positive

she...had a baby...for him...

Katrina K. Guarascio

Existential Bull

On Saturdays,
I play.
Laughing at your bizarre jokes,
making fun of you
while you're not listening,
telling you there is no point,
but continue...continue...continue
I have
drifted into the absurd
and left you
dusty.
While I wait for Godot,
I watch Simpsons reruns,
trying hard to figure out
what motivates Moe,
and plan on
what book to collect
dust on my nightstand next.
I got through three hundred
Pages of Anna Karenina,
but I just don't care anymore.
I sleep with my lights on,
to keep spiders from scratching my eyes.
Night terrors are bad enough
when you are there,

Katrina K. Guarascio

but when no one is

awakened by my screams

it just seems like a waste of time.

Let's dance the way Twain

intended us to.

Let's lie in the gutters

the way Wilde said some

of us already do.

Let's laugh…and laugh…and laugh

As long as this

existential bull crap is here,

we might as well give it a whirl.

DREAMS ON THE PILLOW OF A CRUEL GOD

DREAM I

The woman and man are riding in an old white truck on a rough country road lined with olive trees. The dust hanging in the air is amber and turquoise. The season is indeterminate. What they turn towards is the moon, *La Luna,* clearly seen though it is morning. What they turn from is the memory of villages and obedience, obligations. At trailside, a roan horse is stamping its hooves, impatient to be ridden.

In the open back of the truck they drive is *El Arpa*, a great gold harp lashed to its flatbed, also *El Cazo*, many copper cooking pots. The harp jingles with each jarring of the road, the axle of the truck straining; the shining strings sing in the passing wind. The pots shift, slide, clatter, demand attention.

They are riding in an old white truck on a rough country road lined with olive trees. The man and woman laugh, touch one another in intimate places, stop often to kiss. They brag to each other about how much in love they are.

Their destination is less important than the journey, the way more precious than its end.

I want not to waste myself, she said, offering him *La Pera*, a pear. I want never to complain as we grow old, to age without vanity or regret. I want you to remember how I am today always, he said, remember me just so, that I am brave and careless of consequence.

The woman and man are riding in an old white truck on a rough, country road lined with olive trees. The season is indeterminate. They are neither young nor old. Nearing a river, they hear the songs of *La Rana*, a feast of frogs' voices, the river a complex music that lapses into quiet as they come near.

We are the last and best metaphor, he shouts. Do you believe in me? I have no money but I have everything else to give her. The frogs produce a scale and he lays his heart in it. They give him its measure in coin.

The river and the frogs invite him to say more. The white truck becomes a swan boat. The harp and copper pots tinkle on, though tarnish is setting in. They begin to climb aboard. My soul's work is in hand, he shouts again. This woman gives me what I need. I give him more than he knows, she tells the river, the frogs. If he guesses, he will leave me as a filthy thief.

They are neither young nor old. The season is indeterminate. What she doesn't know, their road ends at the river, their ways go separate from there. He marries another but grieves for her always.

What she doesn't know, the harp is her future, the copper pots her past. When she carries a child she wishes was his, she is frightened at the sight of a white truck.

What he doesn't know, their road ends at the river, their ways go separate from there. Olive trees and the voices of frogs will forever make him weep, for no reason at all.

What he doesn't know, when he sleeps, the woman beside him wears the face of his mother long dead, who means him well.

DREAM II

What is this place? she asks. It seems wrong, so wrong, the starkness, the craggy austerity. Below her a vista shows a long ago dried-up riverbed. This is a land without comfort or gain. Surely it is Unblessed, she thinks, there is no water here.

Alone now but hadn't someone been with her? Yet when
she looked away and back again, he'd gone. Who was he
anyway? Had she imagined him? Worse, had he imagined
her?

She glances down at her hands holding a tarnished pot.
Inside is a wizened but perfect pear. The light shines
through her fingers, shows the outline of bones. Her
fingernails are abalone shells, thin and transparent. That's
not right either, she thinks, my hands are solid, aren't they?

Her belly and chest are dappled with stars. Her breasts
shimmer like freshly blown glass, taken hot from the glory
hole and spun into goblet forms by some artisan god, they
are molten and glistening. No milk could come from such
vessels. Her legs and arms stretch impossibly long, extend
over vast distances, blend into sky. Yes, she is luminous,

perhaps terribly beautiful, but she longs instead to be
substantial, longs to be as she remembers being.

She moves and it is with unintended force. She weeps, her
tears are torrential, wash over the hardened arroyos, cause
the clay hillsides to crack. The river replenishes briefly
then is again parched earth. A sigh is katabatic, becomes
the *Haboob*, a scorpion-tailed wind which strikes as an
immense dust storm, a seemingly impenetrable curtain of
grit towering nearly a mile high. Too much, too much, she

murmurs and her words shatter rock. Her tears become nettles, dropping onto the once again dry land. In the distance, a roan horse canters away.

The expansion stops with a sound of cataclysm. Dispersal begins as she tumbles over and over into space. Her vision melts. Stories are leaving her now, familiar faces, numbers and dates. The color blue is lost forever and so are certain constellations whose names are erased. She reaches towards a grey door that opens and closes, opens again.

Soon she would forget him altogether she fears, whoever he was, even eventually forget herself. She would forget olive trees, harps and copper pots. Forget the music of frogs, the river, the taste of love and pears. Soon, she fears, become a phantasm, a succubus, end as a shadow wraith in another woman's dream.

DREAM III

His new wife cries out in her sleep. He wakes with difficulty, comforts her uneasily, not remembering exactly how she came to be in his bed. He had been dreaming of someone else.

Michelle Holland

Storm Swallowing

I've drunk a hurricane,
not knowing of course,
how to take a storm moderately.

Paper umbrellas take flight,
gusts of ocean breeze erase
any evidence of my footfalls.

Desert dunes grow to meet heavy rain.
Like a wild turkey in the Gila,
I throw my head back and swallow.

I've heard drowning is peaceful.
The water outside becomes the water inside,
and the body balances,
at rest where life began.

I wonder if I'm always drunk,
not knowing of course,
when to stop this breathing in,
this inhalation of all I can take
ahead of me.

Michelle Holland

A shooting star fell out of Orion
just before the turn to Chimayo,
and I almost hit the wandering cows.
My eyes fell from the stars
as I was wishing and met
the road filled with cows'
slow figures in the dark.
I just missed their languid brown eyes
turned to my headlights.

Drink. I drink in stars and cows,
and the long curves of the road home.
I drink storms and red sand hills,
and lose my balance, over and over,
because there is still enough fight in me
to resist drowning altogether.

I feel the pull of the empty road,
I hear the weird winter thunder
that portends God knows what.
So aware I will remain to the line
between light and dark,
the balance of resistance and acceptance,
my mouth open to any storm.

Lonnie Howard

Late August

Egg shells speak to me more clearly now
after visiting my sister. Cucumber peelings,
dry husks of onion, apple core
and basil stems all want to go back
to the earth, to that particular
gravity, to that dark fecundity.

And when I poured the daily scraps
on the compost pile this evening,
tiny ants burst from the old cantaloupe.
They stream out and hurry
away. When I leave they will return
to the business of devouring, return
to the work of transformation.

Her red and orange zinnias
were five feet high. Dahlia explosions
of purple and white taller than I.
We drank color. We feasted
on the fruits. Tomatoes the size of grapefruit,
peppers and herbs in wild profusion;
leafy blooming rip.

Lonnie Howard

Coming from high desert and drought
I could hardly believe the wealth
of this garden. Her grown daughter smiled,
and said *it's the fertilizer*, the ashes
scattered under the tangle of nasturtiums.
The husband and father had put a gun
to his head one day before Thanksgiving,
when the garden was a confusion of brown,
when dried vines and zinnia stalks swayed
in autumn wind. When the earth
was quiet and cold.

They could think of nothing else
to do with him but tuck his ashes in close
to their living and watch him turn his face finally
to the Sun.

Francis Hunter

Mrs. Lot

It was just like him
to wake us before dawn.
"Come on. Get up.
We must go.
No time to pack.
Let's go! Now."
He had been muttering darkly:
the people would be punished
mark his words.
So we were out of town
on the desert road
following the tracks of the camels
to God knows where.
Lot and God weren't telling me.
Lot had the donkey, of course,
and his saddle bags full.
I was on foot like our girls.
They were running ahead;
it was a game to them,
an adventure.
Like all teenagers,
they were moths
drawn to bright lights,
wherever they might be.

Francis Hunter

My heart was heavy,

slowing me down.

My neighbors weren't all bad.

Where was his head?

I had been friends with them

since childhood.

You don't leave friends

without a word.

How could I not look back?

Just once. I looked. Houses,

market, shady palm trees,

children playing outside our home,

women talking at the well.

Lot rode on, not noticing.

They say I turned into a pillar of salt.

They always make up stories for what

they don't want to know.

My heart grew light

as I walked back.

Angela Janda

The Sound Of

To imagine what could have been,
tilt head back, peer past backyard pinwheels,
wind-spun, spinning silence.
The sound of shoulders bent, bowing.

When we take our buckwheat seats, shins asleep
and think one thought together, then
I know it and I know you and I am
where I could always have wanted to have been.
When in the distance the old convent rises,
old home for children, I only say
what I shouldn't: Did you go inside?
          What?
Did you?

Someone built a statue of the Buddha out of snow,
and someone makes her pilgrimage
to offer offerings, to give what is unrecievable:
a glass bead, a rock from the ash of her mother.

If you come from Canada then you know me
and if you lie with shoulder blades etching wings
into the sand, I know you too, and we
can walk to the snow Buddha together.

Angela Janda

Later I will not tell this as it happened
and I will not remember what I tell. I will not
sew your skin together where it has come apart,
where it has fallen to ends-of-calico, scrap fabric
around your middle.

I will kiss you and wonder later what I meant.

Someone will offer pennies,
a garland of winter berries, a sock, a canoe.
Someone will speak the unspeakable: Did you go inside?
       What?
       Did you?

Inside a room the size of a blue whale heart.
Inside a room stacked with boxes from before the war.
Inside a room where I lost an earring, one earring --
evidence of acquiescence, I suppose, evidence of debt --

I sit in crispy thin sin, in the sun of a hotel patio,
I sit shoulder to shoulder with this
rock of your mother's ash,
to your back, your wings spread wide, bent in a bow,
the sound of a bow, the sound of a sin bowing.

Zachary Kluckman

Sparrows Screaming at Black Holes

Lost
in a drift of snow
with one warm finger and no direct line
from home to home,
he draws circles in the windows
of random houses in passing.
Scratching out spirals
meant to imply the shape of eyes
hiding in the pinions,

where he imagines them like galaxies
of stars imploding under pressure.
Giving up radio signals and
the last blue light of dying.
Universal endings spun between
quaking aspen leaves and needles of pine
knotting cones into spirals with small trajectories.
Soundlessly creating life
like children throwing cranberries at shadows.

Dwelling on the absence of sound;
the pattern of beginning lying
in the fallout of autumn;

a small explosion of leaves
exiting the canvas in gusts
that make the trees look like they're breathing.
He's
barely breathing, and the answer's leaving his chest.
If the beginning was a bang, it was
ignited by the wind.

He wonders briefly
if they'll ever call him a constellation,
if his name will ever leave their lips on a breath
the same way.
In the custody of weathered trees
with skin like spinsters,
secretly acknowledging
the thin amount of light that ever finds its way in,
he's standing in the silence between winds
like a small town guarded by forests.
He breathes in the absence,
attempting to become a black hole,
protesting weightlessness.

He stands like Narcissus
frozen with a lust for himself,
half-wilding in restless pursuit of impact.
Running at trees with head down

to find the expansion of dark galaxies

falling into flat discs behind his eyes,

spinning into spirals like fingerprints left on glass.

He's

barely breathing,

and his chest moves

like sparrows screaming at black holes;

flown into windows.

Weightless and waiting

for the wind to stir him

like a leaf spinning into creation;

like a universe waiting for its breath to return.

Borrowed Peace

That lopsided window the one facing south
reflected her glowing sweet memories
memories shaped like peace doves,
a human humming bird feeder
attracting the dead who danced on windowpanes
on nights when she had no tears, or soothing words
to ease overwhelming sadness that cradled
humanity's despair of Bush's cursed war
all those dead babies, mothers' broken hearts
lost children wailing all night desperate forgotten souls
roaming aimlessly nothing will ever be the same again
nothing
just this once she dares to let childhood enter
from a lopsided window he comes her older brother
long dead buried deep in ancient caves at the bottom
of tranquil seas his fingertips emitting pink-purple hues
she wraps her hands around his fingers
glowing with borrowed peace
glowing
drug-induced shadows of yesterday swallow
them into back alleys behind Country Club Market
he was only thirteen, when he stepped into
a hornet's nest of six angry boys his own age
beating up one terrified boy held spread eagle

dozens of on lookers frozen in fear, a few girls
scream when a knife is pulled out but borrowed
peace is growing rapidly in the hands of a
poor barrio boy who isn't afraid
afraid to walk alone to the gang leader to whisper
something in his ear, he holds his hands out
hands shaped like peace doves, the leader
folds his knife gives it to my brother, everyone walks away
for the next seven years of his life he carries
his borrowed peace into schoolyards, back alleys,
barrios, his familia and eventually Viet Nam.

Tonight she is tired of clipping tragedies from newspapers
her fragile heart has forgotten how to dance to live
the world is indifferent, bored, frozen with fear
she wants to release his borrowed innocent peace
let it fly around the universe
flying
breathing hope into a decaying world
that peace is possible, that once a child
a poor barrio boy wasn't afraid to
to look straight into the eyes of violence
wasn't afraid to stop violence
afraid
to hold peace in his tanned hands
to speak gently of a better world

wasn't afraid to cry for injustice / poverty

didn't care what the macho boys thought

tonight she is just a tad selfish instead

she hangs onto his borrowed peace

the way she did when she was little

his little sister

back to when she felt safe, secure / loved

after all she has those kind of hands

the kind that attract the dead.

Jessica Helen Lopez

I'd Love like This if I Were You

If I were a man I would be dashing
Not unlike the silver tip of sword and
the black cloak of Zorro
I, the mustachioed lip of hero and swooning love

If I were a man I'd whisper silvery minnows
That darted like intimate whispers
Into your naked coiled ear of cupped flesh
Silver flashes of true light
I'd waste away in your breath and sweet feminine sweat
I'd gulp your musk from a greedy goblet
I would be the suicidal Romeo of your reverie

If I were a man I would be the woman
You always wanted me to be
The silence that only the trees can bring
When there is no wind to speak of
I'd cradle our babies and become mother
I'd be the father you forever yearned for

I would cup you like a womb and be
The barefoot male divinity
That of brute arm and dark hair

Jessica Helen Lopez

Thick pelvis and broad waist
Ripened shoulder and indestructible Achilles

I'd take my cloak and cover your nakedness
Swash buckle my way into your memory
I'd be Bogart without the ego
Orson Welles without the selfishness
I would color your world with all of
The creative energy I could muster

If I were a man I'd be debonair and strike your fancy
The Laurence Olivier of glittering desert and silk tents
Yellow flapping yards of fabric curling around the breeze
Curling around the dry sun that
festooned your desolate sky

I will tiptoe around your clouds
Offer my sinuous desire and motherly love
I'd smooth the wrinkles from your sad coat
Gorge on your fire and endless listlessness

I am no Diego
I would paint no one but you
Jealous and guarded of your russet form

If I were your man I'd bow my lovely head
Like the soft brow of a velvety doe
I would surrender beneath the fern

Listen to me coo for you like a flock of doves
Like the spent rain over summer mountains
I'd rent a thousand knives of poetry into your quintessence
Sweep over the Mojave as rain does
I would sprout for you
The unexpected green life from the parched
cracked lip of dirt

If I were a man I would clasp you to me
Save myself in a silver locket that
Breathes against your clavicle
And lay like soft metal against the skin over your lungs
The copper taste of kisses beneath the tongue
I'd be your burnt penny
I will be your Lorca

I would be the heart and safe sword that held you
Like I would want to hold myself
If I were a man I would be dashing
The Don Quixote of your afternoon poem
Frail skinny old man with the heart of a golden lion

Jessica Helen Lopez

I would trip over you like a windmill

Paint you like a Spanish cubist

Juxtapose your breasts against the

oil paint of strange angle

The awkward beauty of shape and sharp lines

Drink me like watermelon

Ample flesh and emerald rind

The ruby fruit fashioned from the lovely garden

Of the aged contented wife

Drink me like a garden

I will not elude you

I will toil within you

I will be dashing through and through

Patrick Lopez

Church Merchant

This is for U sleazy so-called, self-proclaimed
Soul saving church merchant
You ball breaking, basket-passing, blasphemy masking
Frequent begging, always asking for the underdog's help
Church merchant.

U smooth talking, sly son-of-a-bitch savior
Selling lies and slots in heaven,
Wheeling and dealing, right-wing loving
Church merchant.

Fuck U fraudulent, foul-mouthed, alter boy fucking
Afterlife judging, crooks with books church merchant.
With your temple of fascists and your war-like tactics,
Belligerent bibles attacking in masses
Dulling my senses,
Church merchant.

You're the wrongful reason Bush was re-elected
Now we're at war, the devil's resurrected
No need 2 save me or my progressive people,
Because poetry is our holy temple,
The mic is my gun,
These lyrics my bullets,
U can never stop a revolution,
Or silence the truest.

Bobbi Lurie

GRAMMAR

We met in the middle of a paragraph
The world is an accident of grammar

I found you my treasure
But treasure is a verb not a noun

And what can I do
Paralyzed like a secret

I call your name
All is illusion (except) (accept) love

Sandra D. Lynn

"I Got Ready to Meet you in your Death…"

I got ready to meet you
in your death.

Drove the long highway
past jukebox lament, broke down towns,
all the abandoned
way home.

       A moon moved casually across the sky,
       erasing heat lightning and wind.

The first night I came home to your death,
the house you built was locked and empty,
and I had no key.
A key on a purple ribbon, somewhere hidden,
but just barely out of sight,
like the doom in your body all these years.

       A mockingbird split the night open.

The key found,
night and your house lay around me,
broken water.

       Out side the bedroom window

in a tree I shaped all night
the mockingbird played,
his many songs
tilling my dreams
with a silver spade.

That night
was pierced
right through with song,
with a glistening
rollicking pain.

I got ready to meet you
in your death,
prepared for its decorum.
but the next night,
I found myself singing by your coffin,
stroking your hair,
still quick with light.

Mockingbird,
many songs.

Lord of Mysteries.

These words were broken over you while
dust lifted on the wind.

Amalio Madueño

Jacona Wind

Divine wind you bring questions for me:
Why do I feel so small in Pojoaque Cemetery
Whom is more numerous, the living or the dead
Is life the opposite of death or of birth
And what about the power of curses

I've been lately amused by dreams of:
A 12-lane coffin expressway
My naked body swarmed by butterflies
Guardians of the dead emerging from the *acequia*
Sudden subsidence of the brain hemorrhage
Patrolling against grave robbers

The sheer numbers, a kind of balance, a ballet
If you will, of the dead & living, the 3rd Law:
A death-life balance not to be created or destroyed.
So many dead, so many equally alive,
New life and its opposite for Eternity.
No "play dead" nonsense, The Continual War
Is our death play, written by the dead for the living.

Mary McGinnis

Prayer After too Much Sugar

God, you could men the cut moon if you would,
you could catch the lizard and turn it blue.

You could make Snow Moon release
like a woman laughing hard.

You could punch clouds,
you could pour small ponds into arroyos.

You could update Rilke,
and make him sexy…

By the way, I am ready for my next life now:
rock star and expert mechanic.

My scream is blue, my arms are thin,
my yawn is bone and snake river.

You can let me make rain;
I will wear the Snow Moon and show her off.

God, this is our doing, our circus,
 it will soon be Tuesday-

time to forgive the knife,
and give the fetus a suitable tank.

Don McIver

The Blank Page

The blank page is undeniably white,

maybe lined,

frayed around the edges

or blue bordered

with common icons.

But the mass of it is blank,

like the night sky is mostly empty, a vacuum,

and the space between nucleus and

orbiting electrons is empty.

As if it too is waiting for me to create upon it.

Nevermind,

that this line doesn't use the full margins,

and this font

means that "O" is set apart by more white than black.

Creativity needs empty space,

a hollow chamber,

a background and a foreground,

a quiet house

with the radio turned off,

the stove simmering brown rice

and the phone messages returned.

Creating poetry is about silence,

Don McIver

not words,

not rhythm, rhyme or conceit,

but listening to silence and plucking the poem

as if it were a blooming dandelion

and blowing parts of it upon this blank page

and hoping some of it would grow.

Dora McQuaid

HE PAINTS BUFFALO

For Paul

When people ask,
Paul tells them he is a painter.

As with everything he applies himself to,
he uses his hands, and leans in from the hip,
into the canvas,
as finger splay invokes image in front of him,
and then in front of us.
I've seen him cook this way, too,
for people he loves,
and he rides and races motorcycles all the same:
All that leaning in, and the spy glass eyes.
Breath moves in and out of him indecipherably,
as though it were only detail,
potential distraction from the momentary prayer.

I lay next to him one morning,
facing his back, both of us on our sides,
endlessly quiet even as we spoke,
barely touching.
In that half-light, wooden slat shades down in late July,
the pulled flesh scars on his shoulder blades
rested in inverted map relief.

Dora McQuaid

My lungs hitched with my heart,
word flash-*torture Vietnam, father's fist,*
jersey boy Friday night street fight-
visceral in my mind's mirror.
I touched the pocks, placed the full whorl of my finger
print and tip into those little beds of whitened skin,
so deep it seemed the possibility of pigment
had been spelt out of the flesh, from the muscle itself.

I hung question at the end of his name:
What or who did this to you?

Ceremony, he said.
Sun dance prayer…
choke cherry stakes on either wing blade,
and rope wound around their apex,
tied to buffalo skulls.
And then I dragged them,
around the circle,
around the compass,
until the skin broke
and the spirit left me.

Why? I asked.
For the buffalo, he said, quietly.
To honor them, for the way we took
their lives.

Dora McQuaid

I rested my fingers in the circles,
knowing the depth of his flesh,
wondering at spirit poured into the sleeve
of gristle and skin, his breath and silence.

This is Paul.
This is how he loves the buffalo.
This is how I have seen him living himself:
Leaning in with his hands,
fiercely, gently, and as focused as a prayer.

Miranda Merklein

Woman, If We All Feel As Ugly,
Who Are The Most Beautiful?

I lay here in the lamplight, afraid to be seen. Or –
if my arm were to fall off the bed and wander to the door
then maybe we could meet
outside

and the coyote with birch wings would not seem so strange
as she winds around these stone-bedded trails.

Through the combed desert landscape
we would use this driving song
to guide us

away from that prickled fruit.

We would follow the musky trail of recognition
to what was forgotten
worlds ago.

Ensnared in twilight, we would smile at each other,
knowing why it never felt right
to be caught.

Miranda Merklein

Apart from ourselves, we see worn and weary
what was woven to opaqueness
by our own bound hands.

It all lies torn and tattered before us,
these fraying unravelments,
It is hard now to imagine how they fastened like a skin.

Love Hurts

My eyes trained on his smooth stub. Chopping wood?
Saving a kitten from a corn combine? Folks call him
Stumpy? Finger Boy? Blood shoot everywhere? Girls
faint? Or wife just said, "Idiot!"

"Sent it to an old love," his pupils dilated with mad
satisfaction. "Sliced it right off. WHACK! Stuck it an
envelope and the stub in hot coals. She jilted me. Hadduh
put pain in perspective. Revenge too."

"Work?"

He fondled the stump, "Guess so, cops ran prints on
the finger I sent. Took my mind off my achin' heart and
she cudn't do her job no more. "

I waited.

"Beauty parlor. Manicurist."

Brion Milar

P'oe Tsawa: Ode to Esther Martinez

The soft words of your native tongue,
spoken gently in the wind,
penetrate the essence of my soul.

Your message is one of Love, Culture,
Family, Tradition, Language.
Life eternal flowed from your lips.
Teach them to speak.
Tewa.
They will listen.

P'oe tsawa.
Beloved teacher.
Your words flow like the river
you loved.

P'oe tsawa.
Beloved story-teller.
Your voice tells the Truth.
The stories you share make the world a better place.

Pehtsiyeh, life's lessons.
Share your knowledge.
Pass it down.
Listen my children.

Brion Milar

Ogedi.
Preserve tradition.
Celebrate culture.
Keep history alive.

Memorias.
Your Spirit.
Your humor.
Your smile.
Grandson is wise.

Wowatsi.
Thank you for sharing your life
with the world outside your own.

Descansa en Paz.
Teacher, Mother, Story-teller, Grandmother.
A new life awaits you.
Sacred Child of the Earth Mother.

Esther Martinez was killed by a drunk driver on the way to her home at San Juan Pueblo after receiving the Arts National Heritage Fellowship from NEA. The 94 years old Martinez had dedicated her life to preserving the Tewa language and culture.

Merimee Moffitt

Iambic Spectrum

I hide in my pretty
I hide in my tender soft
I hide in eyes and teeth
I feed my self
I breathe and walk
I hide in books and dictionaries
I hide in Steinbeck, Lawrence
Kerouac and Brautigan's
wisps of rain and hair
In poems Kool-aid Jell-O
I hide my lost and wandering
I hide my brain and the chess club boys
My pointless breasts and legs and
someone
to be my wall my end stop
I hide in him with him on him
I am nothing but hidden
I hide my panic
The dizzy lost place, space
I hide in harassment like an
amniotic lake I hide in rape
where rape can't touch me
In hate and I float in the water
of hate and birth myself
I eat the placenta alive, the thief

Merimee Moffitt

I take a place and call it mine
Barely my air I smoke so I can see
to feed my son and pay the rent
My son my rent
My feet my breath all mine
I choose to chop ten cords
of wood I hide in mountain woman
In muscle and mad I hide in work
I won't kick your ass
I am strong

I am jars of glistening berries
of Colorado peaches
I am teacher of words
mother of babies maker of
pies and cakes of opinion
I live in adobe snow and light
and in your face

(and those neo-con assholes got
one thing right.

Next time, I'm marrying my dog.)

Carol Moldaw

When It Rains

we must be careful
to admit sadness.
For who is there to reproach us,
with our hearts in the balance?

Tonight it *is* raining.
I eat berries off your tongue.
Your hands join the stream
bathing my breasts.

Rain has no words
to console us, but I catch water
so your mouth will come close
to my cupped palms:

no one ever touched me
pained by such thirst.
Night flocks over us,
and, darker, the rain.

Mary Oishi

I am a Poet

i am a poet

i am a poet to reclaim the ravages of war
to amplify the human heartbeat
in the chest of the enemy
to remind the soldier that he once was a child who
dissolved into tears
at the death of a dog

i am a poet to reclaim the ravages of war
rained by one race, one religion on another
sometimes between nations
sometimes within them
i cut all skins and mingle the red blood indistinguishable
on the page
i fuse all prayers into one chant of longing for a justice, a
goodness
that yet eludes us

i am a poet to reclaim the ravages of war
to pluck the child from beneath
the bruising arm of rage

to pluck the woman
from the path of rape's intruding missile
to hold them up in sun drenched mist
where they can sparkle golden
and untarnished as the day
they burst this world a breath of God

i am a poet to reclaim the humanity from the ravages of
war not to count the casualties but to heal them

i am a poet and my task is immense
i cannot do it alone
but an army of poets can kiss the world awake

Jon Paszkiewicz

Lilacs and Whales

I came tonight
to tell you twenty-one things;

I go to bed with the window open
and wake up when the sun won't let me sleep.

Some of the words you spoke were sung
even though you didn't know what your voice was doing.

The estate that your song created
is a place that I've visited once in prayer
and while there,
the heirs of the breeze ask me
what level of detail I want in my life.
And by passing pollen
I'm asked how much I need.

All of our prayers are always answered;
I believe this to be true because
now, what I feel comes out
before what I think.

Five of twenty one I run like hell from
and one more, I bang my head

against the wheel trying to remember.
You left dents in the dash too.

#7 a lilac bush told me.
She describes a world where people
possessed the power of god and
were made without air and
without water.
Then she spoon fed me frost
and made me keep her secret.

I've held my tongue until right now and
I can still only tell you how
the absence of her affection smoothes my cuts.
Now you can keep my secret.

I've seen how people with symmetry
become forces of nature using
nothing but a decision not to use
indoor voices and breaths encapsulated in bubbles

…and the breaths can be juggled.
And of all of the jugglers the clowns are the greatest.
It's because the clowns have a different rhythm.
The rhythm is sovereign
and can leave you amazed and
the only bubbles that are burst

are the words I've never heard;
which tell me
I need to learn to love the happiness
as much as I love it's pursuit.

I've been ordered to surround myself with inspiration
and when I comply,
I see my soul again
and he's so different from me.

His body has no bones.
He speaks languages that others feel as temperature
and see as color.
He's soft and he's humble and
he knows that tears are gifts to write about;
he laughs and he doesn't forget and
his arms don't attach to his body.
His will is sweet like water and
he loves me.

You need to know that the way I feel walking to you
has to be the way that Clark Kent feels when he
sees a phone booth and hears a scream.
I know that when I step out of the light
you'll remember the look on my face
like what's left after pouring water
over an empty hand.

Jon Paszkiewicz

And the palms of my hands grow roses
whose buds incubate the embryos of whales.
and when the whales bloom
I sail home with them like Jonah;
sleeping until I've arrived
like I've found moiety with
the poppies and the pepper.

Tonight
I can't finish,
because I can't betray the lilac.
I know that she'll find me again.

And it all comes together.

And it was a good taste.

Is that how you see it?

I promise you,
soon.

Me and My Sister

ladies first I say
offering my sister a cup of tea
poured from a bottle of bleach.

don't tell Mom I say to her
after throwing a dart
into her leg.

we are helping daddy load the trailer.
she slices through my eyelid with a flying brick.

toro! toro!
my sister slams the matador's cape of a door
before my charging bull.

my head goes right through the glass.

Jonathon Rollins

The Similarities of Gravity and Love

I wake up every morning
with the expectation that my wife
will have left me.
This way I prepare myself for
what I feel is the inevitable. Fully
aware, on some subconscious level,
that this preparation may inadvertently
spill over into the real world
of cause and effect. Nevertheless,
as consciousness slowly sneaks into
my sleeping life, I lay there in bed,
eyes still closed, and imagine what I
will do if I move my arm over and
the bed is empty. What would be my
first reaction when I open my eyes
and see the note on the pillow?

Or would there even be a note?
Would I simply know she was gone?
Gravity and Love being similar forces,
both invisible phenomena acting on two or
more objects in subtle yet powerful
ways. Because of the curvature of space.
The curvature of souls.

Jonathon Rollins

We can't see the new moon yet the
continual progression of the tides,
the undisturbed rotation of the earth,
assure us that it is there.
But if it were removed, quietly slipped
out of the covers of the Earth, in
the middle of the day, note or not,
we would know it was gone.
The effects of is abandonment
would be immediate, earthquakes, floods,
the lost song of wolves.
In the same way I would know
that she were gone. While an empty
bed could mean a trip to the bathroom,
the kitchen, or many other things,
There would still be something between us.
Unseen, unheard, yet there.
A bond.
A knowing.
Sensed from the subtle play of gravity/love
on my heart, my mind.
If this where removed I would know instantly;
and the effects on the earth would be
laughable in comparison.
But she's always there when I open my eyes,
just like the first time.

Lori Romero

CYCLE OF ECLIPSES

Perfect Persephone,
budding blackberry winter girl
with perfumed spring in her hair
wants to taste what she has never known,
wade in pleasant pools, let Delphian
currents spill over her feet.

She doesn't bother to put on her coat
or tie her scarf. She leaves her room open
to the wind's carousing calloused breath.
The brooding man takes her
down the starless marble aisle
of uncertainty to his kingdom of silent fires.

Straddling a limbo of longing, halfway to hell,
porch and portal fold around her like a shroud.
180 degrees west of sanity,
Persephone looks for the light of day
but finds only darkness.
An eternal cycle of reversal,
each opposite conceives the other,
seeds sowing presence in absence.
From a pomegranate promise,
a dragonfly crawls out of an old earthbound body.

Adam Rubinstein

Courting the Spark

Sometimes the city breathes heavy
down my shirt, the lofts and bars
and office buildings and their loyal suits
and the streets full up with sunshine
and tacky shoes, the women with Yesterday
wrapped around their hips
like the hand of a man who stares back too hard,
the supermarkets unflinching and bereft of tomatoes,
the neighbors' dogs howling their sad and dangerous
music,
the *vatos* who make downtown a funhouse of grease
and belligerent compliments,
the pickups and their rednecks
who drive down my tailbone revving
like their balls were tied & throbbing
to the gas pedal,
the rich houses by the golf course
out watering the lawn at noon with their mechanical
families,
the mile upon mile upon
upon mile of sprawl
that is the city's arms afraid
and ashamed of its heart
or its face,
the businessmen who rise dirty

Adam Rubinstein

every morning to un-write the dance of the dead,

and we are no cleaner than them

and we elect them to glove our hands

in movers' boxes,

the traffic lights that know

precisely when you are approaching,

and the wind that crashes

me into you, cheap hello, cheaper

how are you, full of goodbye & get out of me,

the bars over our windows like snakes' teeth,

the freeways full of dead frogs

croaking their way home,

each standing on another to see where the holdup is,

sometimes the city does this, too,

and bottles her hate

from an exhale

and finds me

in Lowe's on Lomas

in the afternoon

and frowns at me, silly *gavacho*,

holds her shoulders like a falling statue

to my anger,

and I think,

Maybe it's time to move.

Maybe I am a walkway obstruction

in a sea of walkway obstructions

Adam Rubinstein

yearning to swing over Albuquerque
on her countless telephone lines
become the current that travels my voice
to California—
I want to weather the summer of travel,
open my eyes under a different street sign
every five to seven days
and kiss the nape of a city
that will love me hard
as 'Burque
with after-hours bars between her teeth
and an infection
that means we can't play tonight.

C'mon, Albuquerque, bring me back
the stale orange slice of Orlando
the fog & promise & thundering karaoke of Portland
the drunk smirk of Flagstaff
New York and her cement-cracked fingernails
Austin's legendarily stinky feet
bring me Billings, Montana (and the night Slayer played
there)
bring me Texas's arterial language of freeways
bring me Maine's soft interest in its strangers
or just
bring me a Frontier Roll
& don't complain

Adam Rubinstein

if I sleep past eight o'clock.
On Wednesday I am leaving you
to crawl softly back along the tether
I found on my ankle a month ago.
If you love me, 'Burque,
you will kiss me once
like unexpected rain in the night
when I am not looking
or am already
gone.

Miriam Sagan

Take a Left At My Mailbox

Cross Sierra Vista and enter the cul-de-sac

Where the pavement ends

Cross over and down into the acequia full of trash

Where a sodden quilt lies in the middle of where

Stream once moved sand

In eddies. The homeless camp

Disintegrates, only one mattress left

And I'm lecturing my daughter

Who steps back to photograph it

Don't come here alone,

And she retorts: I have since I was eight, and then

It's so peaceful here, but

I hate the fence.

This is no arroyo, cut by rain

But a remnant of man, an irrigation ditch

Now watering detritus, the leftover, cast off,

plastic bags and worse.

From here you can cut

Up behind the Indian School

Past the transformer I didn't even know was there

And come out where there once were tracks

Now just the runners half-buried in soil.

It's Baca Street! We're back

Miriam Sagan

In the neighborhood where my daughter

Immediately becomes lost

I don't get straight streets, she says.

My money's good here, I buy two cups of foamy chai

And look in her face, turning from girl to woman

And want to construct

My map of the lost.

Tony Santiago

Shiny

Mental patients have shiny skin.

This was one of my first observations upon entering the psychiatric hospital in October of 1992. Turned out the air conditioners were weak, but at first, I couldn't help but muse on the theory that at a certain level crazy might just drip from the pores like muscled juice from a Christmas ham.

I met a lot of interesting shiny people, all of whom I felt an instant connection to; as it was we were all mental patients who had anything but mental patience for the place we now called home.

There was Linda, a woman with the mind of a five-year old and all the unconditional love that comes with it. She had to be watched more closely than most of us due to a habit of using her fecal matter to write messages to Jesus on the wall.

Then there was Joey; a young man who was missing an eye because of a gunfight he got into with his best friend over whose favorite football team was better.

I was the boy who counted. Tiles, cracks in the wall, you name it; I'd count it. Sometimes I'd count the cuts on my arms, or rock back and forth for hours at a time, until exhaustion set in and I could count the fences leaping over dead sheep in my mind.

Tony Santiago

We were the crazy ones according to the files the state kept on us, but I soon discovered it was the crooked staff who needed the straightest of jackets. Like Steve, who always enjoyed reminding us kids that he was in control. The jingle-jangle of his keys up and down the tombstone gray halls served as the soundtrack of our misery.

"Tony, stop making the others laugh! This is serious!"

"But Steve, laughter is the best medicine."

"No Tony, you're thinking of pills. Pills will make you better. Count them. Seven every morning. Pills to stop you from rocking, counting, cutting and laughing. Pills are the answer, so stop joking."

At 17 years old, I remember thinking it strange that humor was so unwelcome in a place so many refer to as the "funny farm". Since then, I've learned that over 94% of America's anti-depressants are given to children. Are we medicating our kids because they are sick, or are we sick because we're medicating our kids?

We were the crazy ones because we had panic attacks and shiny skin and wrote our prayers of shit on the walls.

But at least we prayed.

Tony Santiago

I'll always remember Linda's most common prayer.

"Dear God...no more pills today, please."

On the day of my release, I wanted Steve to say "I hope I never see you again"

Instead, he laughed and said, "You'll be back. You're the shiniest."

And he was right. I went back two more times. But who's counting?

Elaine Schwartz

Deluge

Walls sweat rust.
Water, the color of ocher,
puddles the sills.
I find comfort
with my daughter
in the motion
of the old oak rocker.

She nests in my arms,
her frail form swaddled
in a faded baby blanket.
Her fierce dark eyes shrouded
by translucent lids.
Her breath a weak counterpoint
to the rhythmic creaking
of the chair.

My right foot marks
the steady motion
of this undulating journey,
my ears keen to catch
each shallow breath
One shrill cry erupts
from between her pale lips.

Elaine Schwartz

Her dark eyes open.
No light meets my gaze.
Her final breath slips softly
into the humid air,
bursting the dam
of my soul.

Jeanne Shannon

GOING BLIND IN APRIL

Along the brilliant street
in the unbending glare of noon
tall elms sift down
the paper pennies of old bloom
the paper coin of their seed.

Another month, the doctors say,
before the worm eats the last light.

He dreads the fall of dusk and sleep,
afraid that waking will be night.

He hears the crinkled sound
of elm coins falling
in eddying winds among the cars.

He knows
no coin now
can bribe the worm.

Jeanne Shannon

Gold summer comes, and cars

play their zinc music on the boulevards.

He longs for night

when light comes back,

and in long dreams he sees

the crayon colors of the traffic lights,

and paisley dahlias catching fire.

Daniel Solis

Song for Solomon

I take my godson Solomon from his mother's arms.
He is six months old, frisky feisty ready to play.
Within a minute he tears out one of my earrings
tries to eat it then when I stop him,
happily karate-chops me in the face.
We sit, read hop-on pop, talk for a while,
he pulls my locks, yanks my beard, and twists my nose;
he is having a busy day.
We are comfortable in the easy chair.
He starts to drift and I watch the news with the sound
turned down.
Sanitized images of the war;
it could be on ESPN with camo and weapons.
No thump of mortar or
clamor of machine gun,
no heat of desert
or keen of weeping.

Little Solomon makes soft suckling sounds in his sleep and
slowly it surfaces in my soul;
if the world in its terrible dark appetite wants him,
I cannot stop it.
And I am more afraid of this thought than I have ever been
of anything
before.

Daniel Solis

I think of the Palestinian man and boy

who left their house one day to buy a used car.

Father and son on a happy errand that turned into

a fire-fight.

A bullet found the boy

and the day ran red into the hungry desert streets.

In a taxi the father tried to get him to a hospital

but the soldiers at the check point saw the boy and said no.

They would not let them through.

The hospital less than a mile beyond the barricade;

the soldiers smoking, talking, laughing

the father begged

was ignored

he threatened

was watched

he wept

alone.

Did he sing to his son as he died that day?

Did the sounds

catch in his throat

as hope became a song with no words

and a melody he couldn't remember?

And I think,

what if that man were me,

and that boy my Solomon?

What dark unexpected garden in the heart then?

What terrible flowers then?

Nightmare panoply of blossoms

each opening its baleful mouth full of jagged teeth

to whisper

then moan

then chant

one word-

revenge...

...and I know

if that child were the baby boy in my arms now

I know,

I would not be strong enough

to turn away from that evil.

I know,

I would take the vow and make my will

and say

"bring me the vest of plastic explosives, more than one.

This hollow body is strong.

Load me and dress me and send me

to the check point or the crowded market or the wedding,

I have a gift of blood and fire and wailing
to bestow upon you for taking what I loved most."
But I push away these dark imaginings…
I click off the TV and stare into the half-light.
Little Solomon is resting now
and so I try to sing to him.

(Lullaby sung to the tune of Kiane, by Olu Dara)
Oh Solomon,
won't you go
go to sleep my baby boy?
Oh Solomon,
won't you close your eyes?
My little baby boy,
I told you some stories,
then you karate chopped me in the face and tore my
earrings out tonight,
but you just don't want to go to sleep,
its alright…

I hold him tighter-
He breathes softly-
We are in the world.

Dr. Linda Sonna

bury the why

sing of sunbeams   bogs   sage,
dance   in starlight   fog,   rage
at shadows   smog   moon,
leap   stumble   swoon,
turn another leaf   page   corner,
hope   sigh   cry
but bury the why   bury the why
praise spirits sore or soaring
praise laughter fierce or roaring
praise teardrops soft or pouring
praise the journey sacred
praise life

Arthur Sze

The North Window

Before sky lightens to reveal a coyote fence,
he revels in the unseen: a green eel snaps;

javelinas snort; a cougar sips at a stream.
He will not live as if a seine slowly tightens

around them. Though he will never be a beekeeper,
or lepidopterist, or stand at the North Pole,

he might fire raku ware, whisk them to Atitlán,
set yellow irises on the table, raft them

down the Yukon. He revels at the flavor of
thimbleberries in his mouth, how they rivet

at a kiss. In an instant, raku ware and
the Yukon are at his fingertips. As light

traces sky out the north window, he nods:
silver poplars rise and thin to the very twig.

Sal Treppiedi

Eulogy For Syd Barrett

No one could shovel
through the muck
coagulating
behind eyes six feet
from the nearest sign of life.
When a glimmer of movement
surfaced
on psychedelic canvas
you burrowed further into
colorful abyss,
inventing shades
no palette could hold;
riding a twisted steel breeze
through portals
unbeknownst to science.
And since that which is unknown
frightens us, they named it;
seclusion
madness
prison.
Floyd coaxed, you balked.
The luster of art
tarnished by the greed of success.

With the exception of

the momentary smell of breakthrough

your hands were tied

behind your back.

unable to move thoughts

in this plane,

you graciously thanked the world

for accepting your presence

through the fog of LSD existence.

Yet you knew it was pointless.

You were never here.

Through it all

with random precision

and tortured genius,

you laughed hysterically.

Somewhere no one would reach

the madcap laughed

at us.

Kayce Verde

Ignored

After Mary Oliver

The soft animal of my body
crawled out of my left hand.
It knew how fifty percent of anything
could be ignored,
could be taught with one good slap
not to slouch,
with one harsh word
not to growl.

How many grunts turned to lullaby,
impulses to spring taught to shuffle?
How many *that's not nice, not ladylike*
does it take before the fur falls
to the ground and withers?

The animal in me lurks, waiting
but has forgotten what for.
My body has become the wax
museum in which it hides.

What if one little hair remembers,
grows out beyond paraffin and pretense
refusing to be mowed down?
Bring back the lunge, the slink, the slither!

Kayce Verde

Grow out the claws to scratch
beneath the surface.
Let out the *hiss*
longing to be heard!

Israel Wasserstein

The Next Morning

We did not wake in the cold grip of morning,
never suffered side by side
the loneliness of hangover
as black coffee burned our throats.

That night when longing did not unravel
to realization or disappointment,
did you see what I took so long
to discover, that Tantalus' fate

was not all punishment? Though
his tongue burned inside his mouth,
though his lips shriveled and cracked,
to drink was worse, to drink and find

satisfaction a myth. That night
you began to teach me:
to desire is to be unfulfilled, that fullness
empties again and always into hunger.

K.M. White

Thief

A big old crow
flies overhead
hauling off a hunk of bread.
An old man
stands below in anger
Shakes his fist
his thin wrist
at the great black bird
Bring back my bread
His thin voice
hollers   helpless
My supper
Bring back my supper
Legs thinly tremble in a dance
of futile frenzy
Stop thief
Stop
And weary
his rage dissolves
fades
to a very thin
hunger

Rochelle Williams

Teach Me

You said, *teach me to make words sing.*
I took your hand
and put it on the softest,
most amazing skin of my body,
in the curve between rib and hipbone.
I moved your fingers,
slow as unraveled time,
down that wild beautiful dip—
in, up, over, out
to where the bone juts.
Then I pressed a pen
to your hand and said, *write that.*

I said, *teach me to dance.*
You put your mouth on me
where no one had,
unjointing my body limb by limb,
instructing my blood in rhythms
it once knew but had forgotten,
disassembling me
the way water tongues
earth apart.
Then you pressed my feet
to the floor and said, *dance that.*

Anything

(for Steven J. Meyers)

I comment to Naomi Shihab Nye:
I'll do anything for poetry. She nods,
and I revel in the rare moment of being
inherently understood

by this stranger. For poetry,
I will endure the condescension
of a former poet laureate
and his wife. I will tolerate

the poet who arrives so full
of himself, he assumes I will provide
him with copies
of his own books to read from. For poetry,

I will suffer
my college's administration,
and superfluous forms,
saving receipts, writing

reports. I will withstand
falling for men
who write poetry. Because they love

and respect the Word, I believe
that they will respect and love
me. Because I love poetry,
I'll bear the break ups, break
offs, and falling-aparts, which are,

inevitably, so much trickier
with other poets involved.
For poetry, I'll divorce the man
who refuses to allow

poetry into his life. For poetry,
I will endure the pain
of public speaking, the suffocating anxiety
that bolts through my body

every time I botch
an introduction.
For the State of Poetry,
I'll set my own writing

on hold. I'll take
a second job. For poetry,
I'll play the pipe
and line up the mice, or simply
pass the pipe and pray.

Kimberly Williams

Once, poetry saved
my life. Now, I'm its
enduring slave.

                And willingly,

oh, so willingly,
I pay.

Liza Wolff

Juarez's Ghost Army

The women of Juarez are a ghost army
of gathered breath about to spill
bloody secrets of blue veined revenge.

You are poor, but old enough to work
in a plant for *peso* jingle

The week begins;
el lunes.
You straighten your neck a full inch taller.
Purse innocent unpainted *labios*
as you walk through the hiss of "*mamacita*",
approach uncovered shadows.

el martes.
The driver on bus number one looks straight into
your breasts and says "*Buenos dias*"
before he grunts and shifts his cargo
machine into gear and you fall backwards
into strangers who hold onto slippery,
shiny metal bars.

el miercoles.

Your boyfriend tells you

"*Mi amore,* when we're married,

I won't let you work like this,

you won't have to lift a finger outside our *casa.*

A woman's place is in the home and I'll provide for you."

Part of you likes to work with the other *mujeres-*

to hear about their *niños y familias,*

about sloppy serenades by *novios* who think they can sing,

cuentos about relatives who have gone north.

Part of you likes to work, even in long hot

summer hours with your face

sweat sparkled. You feel proud to have work,

to make money for your family, though it's so little

that the debate is on for each *peso.*

el jueves.

You head out for work, your lunch in a thermos, bus fare

in your pocket.

Other women at the *maquiladora* wonder

where you are today.

You never arrive home.

el viernes.

Your mother still sits with candles lit to the *virgencita*

that beg for your return.

A report was made to the police.

One of them asked if you hadn't

run off with your boyfriend

But your *novio* has been there with your mother,

taken the bus routes

to go look for you. He cases Juarez like it were a *pueblito.*

Searches behind every wall, in between every street crack.

el sabado,

in three weeks

you are found

rotten, half buried among dirt and *basura,*

legs broken, bent away from your virgin treasure.

In between nervous *ataques*, your mother holds vigils

where photos and prayers glow by candlelight.

El domingo.

People rise up enraged by the death of one woman.

People rise up enraged by the death of hundreds of women.

The women of Juarez are a ghost army

of gathered breath about to spill

bloody secrets of blue veined revenge.

Mothers stomp their feet.

The answers lie sideways in the gaps between the buttons

on her dress.

Rachelle Woods

Ripening

six serving girls
beneath a fig tree
waiting for fruit to drop

steaming water
Nubian skin
words I can't understand
so old
fire opal
rose petals
women in water whispering
tales of wet weeds
three snake leaves
sunset firecrackers
garnets
seven drops of blood
scarlet fritillary

six serving girls bathing
making peace at the feeder
all the best stars
bright nipples cupped by strong fingers
avalanche of lips
a dare

tattoos and piercings
the proper gauge
improper gaze
no flutter of angry wings
no speed diving jealousy
our new story is oil on skin
blending scents

bonfires on hills
six dancing women
spun from six serving girls
shining with blood of birth
singing loud
swaying out of time
ancient
as thread
as listening
women in water
mists in deserts

gods and women
waiting for figs

Christina Socorro Yovovich

The Name Others Know

Last night I dreamt a name; Heartsease,
a weed growing in hard soil. I pulled me up
by the root, stripped me nameless.
When I woke, I named myself the Pause Between
The First and Second Ring of the Telephone.
Then, after breakfast,
the Sip of Coffee from an Empty Cup.
On my way to the bus stop, I met a man reeling
down the sidewalk. He clutched a red purse.
He leaned in close, boozy breath whispering,
"You're as big as a house." He shouted
"You must have five husbands!
Five Husbands became my brand new name.
I was Five Husbands in Bermuda Shorts and Floppy Hats.
I was Five Husbands Mowing Five Front Lawns.
I was Five Husbands Waiting for the Bus.
Only when I reached my work, did I take on the name
others know. Only when I said hello, good morning,
how are you, did I stop going by Any Name at All.

Ann Applegarth

AN EXCITING NEW PHASE OF LIFE

My medieval mind dwells
increasingly on images of death.
I dress exclusively in black,
carry The Portable Dante in my
apron pocket and clip
strangers' obituaries, pasting them
neatly in a notebook in alphabetical
order for ready reference.

For two hours this morning
I hummed Mozart's Requiem while
contemplating purgatory and the
state of the dead. Then I
tidied the parlor, baked lemon scones,
and invited three of the livelier shades
for afternoon tea.

Whale Hunting

If someone in the village is angry at you and not speaking,
you may ride to the edge of the ice in spring and the whale
hunting captains will be there with their crew, and
aluminum boats pulled behinds snow machines, walrus
intestine waterproofing.

The wives and children will be coming and going with
coffee and reindeer stew and you can shut down your
snow-go and sit at the edge of the ice waving, sipping
coffee, watching the water and ice-pack float by steaming,
and it is spring and the man whom you thought loved you
is angry and not speaking.

The wife of the whaling captain is serving food; the crew
informs you women are not allowed in hunting boats (bad
luck). The oldest son climbs in the hunting skiff this year
for the first time, and that son – who next year, on his 21st
birthday is murdered in Nome and dumped off the jetty –
he shows you, *if you take this wooden oar and press the
rounded end to your ear like this and the flat end into the
sea…*you can stand bent over the edge, listening to the
drifting songs of whales call from the depths of places you
will never see.

Aztatl

No Specific Pause (For Kit Carson and the Tri-Centennial Celebration)

So, at the city red stop light this young cat dressed in old school _pachuco trajes_ pulled up next to my Indian car with all the dents and scrapes and home-made paint job, _toda madre_ in his white Lincoln Continental _coche_ lowered to the max, spinners in motion; a roulette wheel of bling and good fortune. We nodded in recognition, a point of the chin upwards, tex-mex the mix. Seconds later two young _gavachas_ stopped for the red light next to him, making fun of his low-rider stance, shades, clothes _y quien sabe que mas_. When the light turned green to mean vamanos! El vato, (a majik trick worthy of an Academy Award, or at least a fifth bottle of almond tequila, for we did not know from whence it cometh), he launched an empty plastic soda water bottle missile that missed the driver but caught her companion riding shot-gun square on the jibs. The bottle bounced off the dashboard onto the floor. At the next stop light I caught up to him with time to shout across the hundreds of years of intolerance and racism, "good throw _esse!_" He broke out laughing.

Aztatl

The other car caught up to us and I watched as the two cars sped off at the reappearance of the green light to mean go!(into eternity) throwing at each other what each could find inside the car; broken down pens, empty fast food soda cups, pennies, a windshield wiper. I thought to myself "now why can't we all just get along?"

Lonnie Howard

The Offering

You should never have told
me the story
about the poet arriving
naked
at the door
of his beloved, offering
his poetry in trembling hands.

You told me that story
within hours of our meeting.
Now you say go
slow. You say you are shy
and live far away.

But you came into my life
like a great storm –
wind and rain, thunder
and lightning. I say come
now to my door
naked,
clothed only in your poems.

Angela Janda

Headlights and Dirt

It's like death without the body or the night.
You pushed the front page aside and said,

      I'll never drink again.

It's a kind of motherhood. It's like a wing
that begins at the place the pedals meet the rim
on a bicycle side-down at the crossing of Agua Fria
& St. Francis. It's cold water. *La Garza*
leaning to drink.

It is the sound of rabbit feet, of paper flowers,
of a royal-blue 4-door not braking, it is the sound
that doesn't want to sleep.

There is a different kind of time in falling
on the knees of what the red light couldn't stop.

I said,

      Let me be an instrument. Let me believe
that I am not the soldier & let me believe
that I am not the drunk. Let me believe I am not
shoulder-first in asphalt for nothing, but that you are right
when you prophesy my wings.

Angela Janda

I said,

      Let there be death but not a death
without the body and not a death without sound.
I want to be there in the distance between
headlights & dirt. I want to birth angels. I want
to come between two cars colliding until collapse
has left me generous & I can limp my bent wheels
to somewhere like home.

Deanna Sauceda Messenger

The Carpenter

A realm where he could find perfection.
Each piece a different tone, texture, depth.
Each piece bending and arching with a life of its own.
Knotting, twisting on its own history and past.
Each piece stripping a facet of himself.

Peeling, sanding layers,
always revealing delightful surprises.
Reveling in gruesome knurled
rotted twists that resist skill.
Intimacy with wood brought recognition and wealth.
Each piece he caressed and touched.
Hands and sharp edged tools searched
and yearned for the soul.

Oils of his hands penetrated the fibers
and brought forth depth of grain.
His tears salted the sweet perfume of the cut.

Dr. Linda Sonna

The Prophetess

In Honor of Kahlil Gibran

And they said unto her, speak to us of wisdom.
And she said,

Even as a sparrow's wing brushes stillness from the air and
truth is heard,

So, too, from wordless whispers of a heart, may you grow
wise.

Heed the wisdom of seers, but do not seek in them the
well-spring of perfect knowing.
For though their visions may
lead the blind from darkness,
be not like the blind woman who must look to another to
wrench the shadows from her night.
For the light that guides this one to knowledge may lose
the next in a denser fog.

If you wish the guidance of another,
more sagacious soul,
be ever mindful of the words of madmen,

and those the world proclaims as fools.

For they who are not of the world, though in it,

are blessed with clearer vision than the rest.

And though you seek to grow in knowing,

make not a god of wisdom gleaned upon the way,

that you may know the lie hidden at the core of every well-

known truth.

Instead, let your truth be the endless, painful searching that

is the fate

of all the truly wise.

Bad Girl Moon

Poppies are mating in the fields.

We eat tangerines in bed.
Let the juice stain the sheets.
Sing to Ishtar the wanton,
couples in pickup cabs,
men turning cartwheels.

We listen to water,
hail on new leaves.

Old men die.
The cherry tree blooms.

Under 20

New Mexico's talents do not end at any easy borders, including that of age. The state boasts very active slam competitions and teams for students in middle and high school, competing locally and nationally. This community among poets and the eagerness to foster young voices through local events, as well as poets working in the schools, has led to a tremendous collective youth voice, which can be heard clearly in the word-stream that nurtures this desert with sibilant whispers.

The following is a small sampling of this vital youth scene. In an effort to showcase their work photographically, we have not edited these poems. Beginning as early as eight years old and moving upwards; these poets represent the next generation of writers who will play witness to the world around them. We are thrilled to be able to present them here, and give these young voices an ear to hear.

It is difficult

to get the news from poems

yet men die miserably every day

for lack

of what is found there.

-William Carlos Williams

Cathy Abeyta

Untitled

I'm not my hair
I'm not this skin
I'm not your expectations
I'm not my hair,
I'm not my skin
I am my soul
Does the way I wear my hair
Make me a better person
Does the way I wear my hair
Make me a better person

John Kalvin Kluckman

My Shadow

It's dark

A very dark night

I see my reflection in the mirror

It is a monster, I cried

I run faster and faster

For my shadow I have beneath my toes

The sand makes me sink

I yell as my shadow sinks

Julio E. Mendez

Untitled

y las sembras de hoy y manana se estan muriendo,
el hombre no quiere ya no mas,
y me estoy muriendo, pudriendo
?que es el problema? me dice la mente
y pregunto a dios:
ayuda me senor con brazos aviertos
y la mente serada.
y me dice abre los ojos mijo tu tienes vida
y no ay razon para sufrir...------

---

and the seeds of his today and tomorrow are dying,
and this man, I don't want it anymore.
I'm dying myself, rotting.
"So, what's the problem?" my mind asks me,
and I ask God,
Help me Lord with open arms and mind closed.
and He tells me *open your eyes son,*
you have life and no reason to suffer...

Replaced

He stole the parts of my heart
that I clung to so dearly.
He took the last part of my mind.
He took the part of me that screams inside.
He lost the thing I had to find.
I can't stand to look at him, smiling in his head.
I don't know what he is thinking,
but I am wishing that he is dead.
He took, stole, captured their hearts with his greasy smile
of wasted years and dried out tears.
What a transformation.
He was the kid no one knew.
No one I cared about at least.
Then he came back and immediately
crushed the empire I forged.
He destroyed my security and humanity
with a smile.
I know he doesn't realize what it is he has done.
I don't care whether he ever will.
I realize once again that these were not the friends I was
meant to have.
These are not the people
I was supposed to have fun with.
They don't understand the part of me

that I need them to understand.

They don't understand the part of him

that needs to be understood.

One day a choked up kid clinging to his gameboy, the next

he tosses it aside and sticks to stealing happiness.

What a transformation.

I wish they could see his poison

before he slips it into their drinks.

I wish they could stop and see through his lies.

His greasy smile, his tear stained eyes.

He has the board and the strings,

But not the talent or will to learn such things.

Why would he rely on skills he doesn't have, when he

could just lie and have them in his hand.

He doesn't need an angel; he needs a reborn savior, not to

save the remnants of his soul,

but to save us from him.

What a transformation.

Esequiel Acosta a.k.a. "Zeke

THE KID ZEKE

76th street and Hoover
Aka NCT block.
Growin' up pitchin' rocks
San Bernardino be my spot.
I'll never give it up.
Gangs and Drugs keep the streets hot.
Posted up on the block
Waitin' for something to pop off.
Shit started getting hectic
So I tried to stop.

Got a pen and paper and started hip-hop.
Sketchy at first.
Off track and off line.
Thought it was my time to shine.

Homies callin' me sayin',
I need you there tonight
So I jump in the whip.
When I'll be back,
I don't know when.
Villains going through my head.
Wonderin' what would happen if I end up dead.

Esequiel Acosta a.k.a. "Zeke

Snap back to where I started at,

Gun shots got me havin' panic attacks.

Lookin' around and jumpin' to the closest branch.

Sneak to the back of a pad,

Known in the streets as the bad kid.

Jump out the back and unload a clip.

One man shot in the arm,

The rest missed.

Two, three,

Moved to New Mex

At night I pray to god to forgive my sins.

And that's the story of Zeke,

Been taught by the streets,

To all the homies dead, rest in peace.

Author Biographies

Esequiel "Chuco" Acosta a.k.a. "Zeke", is currently a sophomore at Robert F. Kennedy Charter School. Zeke was born in San Bernadino, California, and grew up in South Central L.A, before he moved to Albuquerque. Zeke is a dancer, poet, and rapper, with aspirations of a recording career. He first would like to finish school, and then go back to L.A. to attend the University of Southern California.

Ann Applegarth was awarded an Academy of American Poets prize at the University of New Mexico in 1980. Her work has appeared in print and online publications, including *Sin Fronteras, West Wind Review, Christianity & Literature, St. Anthony Messenger,* and *Lunarosity,* and anthologized in *Shadow and Light: Literature and the Life of Faith.* She lives and writes in Roswell, New Mexico.

Originally from Poulsbo, WA, Tani Arness has been residing in Albuquerque, NM for the past 8 years. She has published in several literary magazines including *Santa Clara Review, Rhino & Green Mountains Review.* Her book, *Iinruq: The Spirit That is In All Things,* is forthcoming from Silver Woods Press.

Aztatl (Jose Garza) was born in San Antonio, Texas of Coahuila and Xikano ancestry. He majored in Sociology and English at Wayne County Community College and Wayne State University. He worked as a social worker and community organizer for 24 years in Detroit, where he was also a union organizer, as well as being active in the Migrant Labor Movement in Ohio and Michigan. Aztatl has taught creative writing and visual art. He has been published more than 40 times, including; Storm Belt #1, Gatherings, and Returning the Gift: Poetry and Prose From the 1st North American Native Writers' Festival, among others.

Jan Marie Baca has been published in various local and online poetry publications, including *Central Avenue*. She has also written an award-winning short fiction piece published in the *Alibi* and is planning on entering the children's fiction market this year. She currently resides in Albuquerque with her husband, two children, three dogs, and a cat.

Jimmy Santiago Baca was born in New Mexico of Indio-Mexican descent. After being sentenced to five years in a maximum security prison, he began to turn his life around: learning to read and write and unearthing a voracious passion for poetry. During a fateful conflict with another inmate, Jimmy was shaken by the voices of Neruda and Lorca, and made a choice that would alter his destiny. Instead of becoming a hardened criminal, he emerged from prison a writer. He published *"Immigrants in Our Own Land"* in 1979, the year he was released from prison. Baca is a winner of the Pushcart Prize, the American Book Award, the International Hispanic Heritage Award and for his memoir *"A Place to Stand"*; the prestigious International Award. In 2006 he won the Cornelius P. Turner Award. Baca has devoted his post-prison life to writing and teaching others who are overcoming hardship. In 2005 he created Cedar Tree Inc., a nonprofit foundation that works to give people of all walks of life the opportunity to become educated and improve their lives. Baca is currently finishing a novel, a play and three poetry manuscripts to be published in 2007. He is also producing a two hour documentary about the power of literature and how it can change lives.

Ray Michael Baca was born in Albuquerque, New Mexico in 1959, and grew up in the small town of Bernalillo. He attended Navajo Community College in Tsaile, Arizona, and Regis University in Denver, Colorado, and since 1981 has made his career in the business sector. Baca has been a guest lecturer at the National Hispanic Cultural Center's, History and Literary Arts, Meet the Writer's Series, October 12, 2005 as well as at the University of New Mexico-Los Alamos library, April 11, 2006. Baca's novel, *"Brotherhood of the Light"* about the Penitente's and Sephardic Crypto-Jews of New Mexico was published by Floricanto Press in 2005. For more on Baca's work, visit raybacabooks.com.

David Baker, currently in exile in Nevada, was born at the old St. Vincent's Hospital in Santa Fe. He has lived at various times, for various lengths, in Taos, Tesuque, Cerrillos, Madrid and Santa Fe. Baker is a former construction worker who decided after 14 years, to put down his wireman's pliers and take up the pen. He has been published in *The Pahrump Valley Times, Skyline Poetry's '06 Autumn Edition of Poetry Express*. Baker is a contract writer and photographer with *The Pahrump Valley Times*. Baker calls his wife his hero for making it possible for him to become a writer/poet. He also feels fortunate to be the hero to one little five year old girl. Baker is overjoyed to have found poetry, which condenses the human experience down to a few essential lines that make those human experiences tangible and real.

Leslie Bentley, PhD., is a writer, personal caregiver, and Reiki practitioner. She has taught theatre and performance studies, been a Boston barista, and has peddled encyclopedias door-to-door. Bentley is an avid New Mexico hiker and unstoppable rock-hound. Her poetry has appeared in *Bulkhead, Central Avenue*, and *The Nebraska Territory*.

Janet K. Brennan, AKA J. B. Stillwater, is a writer and poet living in the foothills of Albuquerque's Sandia Mountains with her husband, Arthur, and a great gray cat named Amos. Her short stories and poetry have been published around the world. Most recently, "*Taj Mahal*

Review," December, 2004, and June, 2005. "*Insights, a Collection of Contemporary Short Stories,*" Dec, 2004 where she is listed as "one of the best contemporary writers of our time.", as well as the "International Who's Who in Poetry", 2004. She also publishes colored pencil art-work and photography, and is currently writing book and manuscript reviews from authors around the globe. Janet has just completed a novel entitled "A Dance in the Woods", and is critically acclaimed for "The Harriet Murphy Stories" Janet and her husband own a greeting card business, named Pearls Designs.

Debbi Brody co-owns and operates Canyon Road Contemporary Art, in Santa Fe, NM. She publishes her poems frequently in *Central Avenue*. Her work has appeared in the Broomweed Journal, Poetica and other national literary magazines. Her latest book, *Portraits in Poetry*, (Village Books Press, Oklahoma, 2006), as well as her chapbook, *FREEFORM*, are available through artqueen58@aol.com. Debbi enjoys hearing from her readers at the above e-mail address as well.

Priscilla Baca y Candelaria is a founding member of the Poetic Justice Institute, and a poet-educator-recording artist. Priscilla appears in the 2006 documentary film Committing Poetry in Times of War (www.committingpoetry.com). Baca y Candelaria is a 29 year veteran public school teacher in New Mexico, still teaching in the Los Lunas area. Mentored by

internationally acclaimed New Mexico author Rudolfo
Anaya, Baca y Candelaria earned her Bachelors and
Masters degrees from UNM. A Spanish language and
Chicana cultural activist, published and performing poet
and recording artist ("*Duende*", her spoken word cd
featuring the music of Christian Orellana), she is also a
nationally published journalist and photographer
(www.zmag.org, www.abqarts.com,
www.hyperactivemusicmagazine.com and in *TM* and *bello*
magazines, among others). Baca y Candelaria teaches via
art, dance, story telling and poetry. She also created and
taught in the innovative and highly successful *Writing
Works* program, with Jimmy Santiago Baca and Bill
Nevins, for the University of New Mexico in 1999-
2000. Priscilla Baca y Candelaria is a lifelong, dedicated
advocate of peace. Her poetry has been published in *Maple
Leaf Rag, Central Avenue* and many other collections. She
is available for readings, lectures and workshops at
sisoy2003@yahool.com

Hakim Bellamy is a still finding his way. In the process,
performance poetry bumped into him in Albuquerque two
years ago. Before that he was a Microbiologist at a Fortune
500 Drug Company and a Junior College Soccer Coach in
South Jersey. Since then, a Grad Student in
Communications in Journalism at UNM, a radio journalist
at KUNM 89.9FM, a Floor Tech at KOB-TV/NBC
Channel 4 in the "Duke City", a performance poetry coach
at South Valley Academy, an Albuquerque City Slam

Champ (2005), 2-Time UNM Word Revolution (Now LOBOSLAM) Champ and a member of 2 National Champion Poetry Teams (Team Albuquerque NPS 2005 & Team UNM CUPSI 2006). Find out more about him at www.digiflowz.net or www.myspace.com/hakimbellamyazhizelf.

Ben Bormann was born on the mesa, and grew in the desert's valley. He left when he got big enough, but came back. Twice. Bormann says, "This place is holy. This place is home."

Ioanna Carlsen's poems have appeared in Poetry, Blue Mesa Review, *Field* and *Chelsea*.

Ana Castillo has written 17 books in various genres, the most noted being her novels *Peel My Love Like an Onion* and *So Far From God.* Her most recent books are the novel-in-verse *Watercolor Women Opaque Men* and the play *Psst... I Have Something to Tell You, Mi Amor.* Her poetry has been collected in the volumes *My Father Was a Toltec* and *I Ask the Impossible.* She edited a collection of essays on Guadalupe-Tonantzin, Goddess of the Americas/La Diosa De Las Américas : Writings on the Virgin of Guadalupe, and has also written essays and columns for newspapers and magazines across the country on various topics such as the murder of Tejano singer, Selena; gender roles in the Farmworkers movement; being a mother; and Feministas turning 50. She has been profiled

and interviewed on National Public Radio and the History Channel. She received an American Book Award from the Before Columbus Foundation for her first novel, *The Mixquiahuala Letters*. Other awards include a Carl Sandburg Award, a Mountains and Plains Booksellers Award, and fellowships from the National Endowment for the Arts in fiction and poetry. She was also awarded a 1998 Sor Juana Achievement Award by the Mexican Fine Arts Center Museum in Chicago. Born in
Chicago of working class parents, she went on to earn an M.A. from the University of Chicago and a Ph.D. in American Studies from the University of Bremen in Germany. Both as a journalist and literary author, she has been a major force in the struggle for economic justice, women's rights and civil liberties. She now makes her permanent home in La Union, New Mexico. Her latest novel, *The Guardians*, will be published in the summer of 2007 by Random House.

Inara Cedrins is new to Albuquerque, returning to America after eight years. An artist, writer and translator, she went to Beijing in 1998 to learn to paint on silk, and remained in China for five years teaching writing and lecturing on art at universities including Tsinghua University and Peking University, as well as the People's Liberation Army. Cedrins had two chapbooks of poetry published by the Chinese Literature Press in Beijing, about China and Egypt: she planned to follow these with one focusing on India (*Honey Water in the Harsh Palace*, completed) and one on Nepal (*Sky Womb*, in progress). Cedrins is a translator of Latvian, her first language, and has used these skills to teach Creative Writing at the University of Latvia, starting a literary agency called The Baltic Edge. Cedrins is currently developing an anthology of Baltic poetry. Also in the works is her anthology of contemporary Chinese poetry, as well as short stories and a trilogy of novels based on her experiences. The first of these, *"The Hotel Sunshine"*, will be published by Petergailis in Riga and will be translated into Latvian. Her most recent book of poetry is *Fugitive Connections*, just published by the Virtual Artists Collaborative in Chicago. Her first anthology of contemporary Latvian poetry was published by the University of Iowa Press in 1981; her chapbook of translations of the poetry of Astrid Ivask, *At the Fallow's Edge*, was a Small Press Book of the Month Club selection and went into a second edition. She has had poems, stories and translations from the Latvian in *the North American Review, Chelsea, Prairie Schooner, the Portland Int'l. Review, The Ledge, The Minnesota Review, Translation/Columbia University, the Massachusetts Review, Kansas Quarterly, The Atlanta Review, New Letters and The Chariton Review*, among others.

Sandra Cisneros was born in Chicago in 1954, the third child and only daughter in a family of seven children. She studied at Loyola University of Chicago (B.A. English 1976) and the University of Iowa (M.F.A. Creative Writing 1978). Her books include a chapbook of poetry,

Bad Boys (Mango Press 1980); two full-length poetry books, *My Wicked Wicked Ways* (Third Woman 1987, Random House 1992) and *Loose Woman* (Alfred A. Knopf 1994); a collection of stories, *Woman Hollering Creek and Other Stories* (Random House 1991); a children's book, *Hairs/Pelitos* (Alfred A. Knopf 1994); and two novels, *The House on Mango Street* (Vintage 1991) and *Caramelo* (Knopf 2002). Her books have won numerous awards and critical acclaim, as well as being translated into over a dozen languages. *House on Mango Street* alone sold over three million copies and is required reading in classrooms across the country, including elementary, middle, high school, and university-level. Other awards include the prestigious MacArthur Foundation Fellowship, 1995; a Texas Medal of the Arts Award, 2003; an honorary Doctor of Humane Letters from Loyola University, Chicago, 2002; and an honorary Doctor of Letters from the State University of New York at Purchase, as well as many others. After past careers as a teacher and counselor to high-school dropouts, an artist-in-the schools where she taught creative writing, a college recruiter, an arts administrator, and a visiting writer at a number of universities, Cisneros currently earns her living by the pen. Cisneros lives in San Antonio, Texas, in a violet house filled with many creatures, little and large.

Kathleen Clute grew up loving sound and rhythms and has turned that into a career as an award-winning composer and pianist. Early in life she discovered that words also

have rhythm and she began writing poetry and lyrics in
middle school. Kathleen has been known to collect words,
and her favorite word is...oohh, no can't tell you that —
she'd have to change all her passwords! She lives south
of Mountainair with her husband, two cats, two horses, and
the endless New Mexico sky.

Carlos Contreras, is a poet, educator, son, lover and
dreamer. A three time member of Albuquerque Slam
teams, he is also a one time college national champion.
Contreras is the 2005 National Poetry Slam Champion and
founder of a grassroots production company with a focus
on youth advocacy (immastar productions, immastar.com).
Contreras has plans for a future in teaching and writing,
but most of all he wants to stay true to himself.

Wayne Crawford lives in Las Cruces, NM, where he
manages the online journal, *Lunarosity*, and is co-
managing editor of the regional anthology, *Sin
Fronteras/Writers Without Borders*. His most
recent collection is "*The Corner of Clark and Kent*"
(Mesilla Valley Press 2004).

Jasmine Cuffee, recently crowned Albuquerque poetry
slam champ of 2007, has been a member of the poetry
community for six years. She was the youth city champ in
2005 and was also a member of the 2004 team that went to
St. Louis. She is the current host of the longest running
slam in Albuquerque at the Blue Dragon Coffeehouse

every second Friday of every month. Jazz, as she's known, would like to invite you to come out and see the show.

Janet Eigner- Lover of the natural world, dance writer, psychologist, mother, wife, grandmother, celebrating four generations of splendid family, extended family, and soul-friends. Selected publications include: *Blue Mesa, Drum Voices Review, Eyeball, Hawaii Review, Manzanita, Mudfish, Natural Bridge, Sagarin Anthology, Reconstructionist, Collected Poems (forthcoming): Still, Life With Datura Visions International, Dance Magazine, Dance Critics of America, St. Louis POST DISPATCH, Santa Fe NEW MEXICAN, Santa Fe REPORTER, THE Magazine, High Altitude Dance.* Selected readings: PEN International, Writers' Voice National Reading Series, River Styx, Edison Theatre - Washington University, Inn at Loretto, Santa Fe Public Library.

Damien Flores hails from Old Town, Albuquerque, NM where he works as a youth advocate. He was a member of the 2004 and 2006 Albuquerque Poetry Slam Teams. Flores has performed across the nation and his collection of poetry, *A Novena of Mud*, was published in 2006 by Destructible Heart Press.

Leslie Fox grew up in New Mexico and completed her MFA in Creative Writing at the University of New Mexico this fall. She placed in the 2001 Mainstream Novel section of the Southwest Writers annual contest. She was awarded a Predator Press Fellowship in 2005, and was a finalist in the Rick DeMarinis Short Fiction Award, 2006. Her stories have appeared in *Medical Muse* and *red. a journal of arts.*

Lee Francis is a poet, performer and activist for educational reform. His work has appeared in Words on a Wire, Native Realities, Native Time and various other publications. He is a member of the 2006 Albuquerque Poetry Slam Team and is the National Director of Wordcraft Circle, a Native American leadership organization. He currently lives in Albuquerque with his crazy dog.

Teresa E. Gallion has published in the *Rag, Willow Street, Central Avenue, Harvard Review, Broomweed Journal, Ghost Ranch Anthologies* and three CD anthologies. She published her first chapbook, *"Walking Sacred Ground (Celebrating the Landscape")* in 2003. She has been a featured reader at local coffee houses and art galleries, the Route 66 Festival in 2001 and the Oklahoma National Poetry Month Celebration in Cheyenne, Oklahoma in 2004. Writing is a spiritual journey for Teresa. When she is not writing, she spends time with her first love, hiking the mountains and deserts of New Mexico.

Bill Gambling is a retired artist and art professor of 29 years. Gambling has worked in many media. Born in Boise, Idaho, he received his BFA from Pratt Institute and moved from Chapel Hill, North Carolina to Las Cruces, New Mexico in 1991.

Lisa Gill is the author of *Red as a Lotus: Letters to a Dead Trappist* (La Alameda, 2002) and *Mortar & Pestle* (New Rivers Press 2006). She received a 2007 National Endowment for the Arts Fellowship in Poetry.

Gary Glazner is the Managing Director for Bowery Arts and Science, the non-profit wing of the Bowery Poetry Club, in New York City. Glazner's work has been featured on NBC's "Today" show, NPR's "All Things Considered" and underwater on the Bay Area Rapid Transit. Glazner is the founder and executive director of the Alzheimer's Poetry Project. For more info go to alzpoetry.com. He is the author of "How to Make a Living as a Poet," on Soft Skull Press.

Katrina K Guarascio lives in Albuquerque, New Mexico where she is working on her Master's degree in Secondary Education at the University of New Mexico. She also works as an instructional aid for developmental English students at Central New Mexico Community College. Her poetry has been published in many literary magazines and e-zines, including *Chantarelle's Notebook, Nerve Cowboy, and Whistling Shade*. She has contributed poetry, short stories, and editorial duties for the Community College's Literary Magazine, *Leonardo,* and the University of New Mexico's Literary Magazine, *Conceptions Southwest*.

Dale Harris edits and publishes *Central Avenue,* a monthly poetry journal that sponsors regular open mic readings in Albuquerque. A native of Colorado who lived in Miami, Fla. for many years, she has made her home in Central New Mexico since 1993. She organizes the popular yearly Poets & Writers Picnic in Mountainair, NM, produces a poetry based variety show in honor of National Poetry Month at the Harwood Art Center and performs her poetry at regional poetry festivals such as Sparrows and Festival of The Imagination, often collaborating with musicians and dancers. Publication includes *The Practice of Peace,* Sherman Asher Press, and *Harwood Anthology,* Old School Books, 2006. Her poetry& music CDs are available online at CD Baby. Dale is also a potter and a nurse practitioner working in the HIV field.

Michelle Holland lives in an old adobe farm house in Chimayo, with her husband and visual artist, Tom Holland, their thirteen-year old daughter Sylvia, and a mess of livestock. Her poetry has been anthologized in *The Harwood Anthology* (Old School Books), *Mirror, Mirror: Reflections on the Way We Look* (Midmarch Arts Press), *Shine on You Crazy Diamond* (Sunstone Press), *The Practice of Peace, and Written with a Spoon: A Poet's Cookbook* (both Sherman Asher Publishing), and she has poetry and creative non-fiction published in *Puerto Del Sol, Manzanita Quarterly, Journal of New Jersey Poets,* and *Fishdrum,* among other literary journals. The

University of South Carolina's Palanquin Press published her first collection of poems, *Love in the Real World*, (1999). Her second collection of poetry, *Event Horizon*, is included in the new Tres Chicas Press publication, *The Sound a Raven Makes*. She is a the treasurer on the board of New Mexico Literary Arts, and an active member of Sin Fronteras/Writers without Borders, as co-poetry editor of the Sin Fronteras Journal, as well as New Mexico Culturenet's Poetry-in-the-Schools coordinator for the Santa Fe Public School System.

Lonnie Howard has lived in Santa Fe since 1981 and is the director of the Scherer Institute of Natural Healing. She began writing poetry in 2000 when a chance encounter introduced her to the poet within. Her work has appeared in *Manzanita Quarterly, Edgz, Spillway Review, Passager, Santa Fe Literary Review*, and as part of a commissioned piece for the Santa Fe Women's Ensemble 2006 Christmas Concert. She is also an avid birder.

Frances Hunter is happy to have put down roots in Santa Fe since 1997 when she arrived after a lifetime of travel. She enjoys the company of family and friends. Her poems have appeared in journals and anthologies in South Africa and America, and she has two published collections, "*A Maverick Elation*" and "*Sesame.*"

Angela Janda, a Minnesotan by birth, has spent the last two and a half years doing theater and writing poetry in

Santa Fe, New Mexico. Her work has appeared in *Central Avenue* and she has staged poetry performances at Theaterwork in Santa Fe, where she is a member of the permanent company. Ms. Janda was the recipient of a 2006 New Mexico Discovery Award for poetry. She can be contacted at ajanda@gmail.com.

Zachary Kluckman lives in a state of animated suspension in Albuquerque, NM, where he operates a monthly poetry workshop, produces poetry for television and occasionally co-ordinates poetry segments for radio as well. Kluckman is a prolific, often experimental poet striving to ride the axis between traditional and performance poetry styles. Kluckman has a nervous habit of pasting stamps on return envelopes upside down to make rejection letters from editors more difficult to send. He also organizes events, runs NM Poetry Tangents and is preparing to assist with fund-raising for other non-profit agencies as well. Kluckman can be seen in a number of film and television roles, and is currently ranked as one of Albuquerque's top ten slam poets. Kluckman has been a featured reader in Chicago and has been published many times locally and nationally. Recent publications include *The Dos Passos Review, The Green Muse, The Quill, Dance to Death,* and the anthologies *American Open Mike (Volumes 1* and *2),* and *A Walk Along the River; A Literary Anthology from the Upper Rio Grande.* Kluckman's first chap-book, "*Per-City Poems*" recently received glowing reviews as well, prompting him to begin work on a second chap-book for release in late 2007. When he is not wallowing in the Bohemian lifestyle that he imagines within an overly fertile mind, Kluckman assumes his secret identity as husband and father to four beautiful children. His ongoing projects can be seen on http://wwwnmpoetrytangents.com, where he wears a goofy hat as poetry editor when he is not practicing primal screaming in artesian wells.

María L. Leyba's (Albuquerque, NM) poetry and literary works spring from her pain growing up in the State Penitentiary and in the barrio of Barelas. Her only son is presently incarcerated in the New Mexico State Penitentiary, and she is determined to help young people stay out of prison. The effects of having a loved one incarcerated are devastating. Leyba is also the editor of "*Angel Dreams*" an anthology of young voices from New Mexico ranging in age from 6 to 18. She has spent many volunteer hours working with youths at risk and incarcerated youths. She has also hosted art & poetry venues for families who have loved ones incarcerated and prisoners throughout New Mexico and been a guest speaker at Highlands University talking about her poetry and prison reform. During the day she's an early childhood educator. Maria says, "Guiding and nurturing very young children brings peace to my heart and makes my world complete."

Jessica Helen Lopez is a member of the 2006

Albuquerque City Slam Team. A new slammer, she has performed in a variety of local and southwestern venues, including a featured solo performance at the District Bar & Grill. Lopez recently completed a competitive team tour throughout the state of Texas that concluded at the National Slam Finals in the weird and beautiful city of Austin. Lopez is a self-described "confessional poet," and has at least twice cried on stage. She refuses to be embarrassed by this and continues to spit rhyme with emotion. Jessica is a single mother, a creative writing student at the University of New Mexico and a waitress trying to stretch a dollar out of fifteen cents. Although dirt poor she is very much content to be writing in the "poor man's field" of poetry until her winning lottery ticket comes through. She does not buy lottery tickets. Lopez has been published in the *American Open Mic Vol 1 Poetry Anthology* and such 'zines as *Central Avenue, the Rag, Feminism Now, TVI Leonardo Anthology* and *Instant Pussy*. Her published work can also be found in the 2006 Slam Team poetry compilation, *Album Familiar* as well as her recorded works, *Live at the Outpost CD Vol 1*. She is the co-founder of the writing workshop and online organization New Mexico Poetry Tangents and continues to perform and write poetry, as well as volunteering within the Albuquerque public school system.

Bobbi Lurie is the author of two poetry collections: *Letter from the Lawn* (Customwords, 2006) and *The Book I Never Read* (CustomWords, 2003). Her work has appeared in numerous literary journals including *The American Poetry Review, New American Writing, Gulf Coast, Puerto del Sol* and *Nimrod*. She lives in Corrales, New Mexico.

Sandra Lynn published her first poem in 1974, and since then has published numerous poems in literary magazines, anthologies, and three books: *I Must Hold These Strangers* (1980), *Three Texas Poets* (1986), and *Where Rainbows Wait for Rain* (1989). In 1982 she won the Dobie Paisano Fellowship Award from the Texas Institute of Letters and was able to live on J. Frank Dobie's ranch in Central Texas and work for six months on the manuscript of Rainbows. She taught creative writing at the O. Henry Museum in Austin, Texas, and at the University of New Mexico's Taos Summer Writers Conference. Since 1989 she has written little poetry and spent her writing time working on nonfiction—articles, essays, and a book about New Mexico history—but her poetry muse has returned recently from a long vacation and stirred up some new poems.

Amalio Madueño lives in Taos, New Mexico. Long associated with the Taos Poetry Circus and Mexican Bob's Poetry Camp, he has published widely in journals across the United States and Europe. Recent anthologies featuring his work include *Venus in the Badlands* (J. Macker, ed. Desert Shovel, Santa Fe 2006) *The 315Experiment* (Dinsmore & Alley, eds., Vancouver 2006) and *Wandering Hermit Review* (Seattle, 2006), *Muse6* (L. Council ed. El Paso, 2006) and *Askew*, Volume 2, 2006 (Ventura, CA).

His latest book of poems, *Lost in the Chamiso*, appeared in 2006 from Wild Embers Press, Ashland, OR. He performs his work regularly throughout New Mexico and the west in featured readings, seminars, television & radio, as well as on videos and CDs.

Mary McGinnis has been living, writing, eating sweet things, and pondering about God in New Mexico since 1972. Her first full-length collection, *"Listening For Cactus"*, was published in 1997. Her work has been anthologized, and she is a frequent contributor to *The Rag* and *Central Avenue*, as well as performing in Santa Fe.

Don McIver currently lives in Albuquerque, New Mexico. He is the author of *"The Noisy Pen*," a 3 time member of the ABQ Slam Team, an award winning radio producer, the media director for the 2005 National Poetry Slam (the largest poetry slam in history), the media director for the Alzheimer's Poetry Project, and a Trustee on the Executive Council for Poetry Slam Incorporated. He's the slam master for Albuquerque, where he curates a monthly reading, and hosts Poetry & Beer (the longest continually running poetry reading in New Mexico). McIver has hosted a variety of fundraising events for Healthcare for the Homeless, the Alliance for Academic Freedom, and Poets Against the War, among others. He's read across the United States, including; New York City, Los Angeles, Chicago, Phoenix, Denver, and all over New Mexico. McIver is widely published and has read poetry for a variety of audiences from elementary schools to universities, in churches and bars, for pay and for free. For more information, please visit www.donmciver.net.

Dora E. McQuaid descends from traveling gypsies, Irish Golden-gloved boxers, and strong women, whose stories prompted her fascination with the written and spoken word. In addition to teaching in the Department of Communication Arts and Sciences at Penn State, McQuaid combines her passion for language and performance with her dedication to activism to raise awareness of the issues of domestic and sexual violence, and to teaching writing and performance as means of empowerment. For her efforts, Dora was awarded the Fifth Annual Pennsylvania Governor's Victim Services Pathfinder Award in 2003 for her activism and advocacy on behalf of victims and survivors of domestic and sexual violence. She was recognized by the Pennsylvania Senate in 2003 for her activism efforts and her contributions to the state of Pennsylvania. Dora was chosen as a 2005 Vagina Warrior Honoree by the cast members of the Penn State Production of Eve Ensler's play, The Vagina Monologues. Kate Bogle's short film, "One Woman's Voice," which documents Dora's combined roles of poet, teacher, activist and survivor, is available through Penn State Public Broadcasting. Dora is featured in Suzanne Keller's book, Free Spirits, and her image is soon to appear in Mike Pilato's State College Public Mural Project, Inspirations. Dora has lent art to activism for an array of organizations and events, including writing the commissioned poster poem, "Around This Table," to commemorate the 25th Anniversary of The Pennsylvania Coalition Against Domestic Violence, speaking, by invitation, to the PA Supreme Court Subcommittee on Racial and Gender Bias in the Judicial System, and performing in the Penn State production of The Vagina Monologues and Take Back The Night Rallies, in addition to other events. Her work has been incorporated into plays, films, musical compositions, books, course readings, newsletters, and domestic violence programs and vigils. Currently, Dora is collaborating with an array of artists, and touring internationally with the all-woman poetry and performance troupe, the Neo-Spinsters, which she co-founded with Pat Payne. In 2006, Dora served as Poet-In-residence at The Harwood Museum of Art in Taos, New Mexico, where she finished (finally!) her next collection of poems.

B. Joseph McQueen left the U.S. Postal Service in 2003 after 17 years to paint full-time. He lives in Santa Fe with his wife and beloved animals.
Please visit his on-line portfolio at: www.highbelow.com

Julio Mendez, is currently a senior at Albuquerque's Robert F. Kennedy Charter School. Julio is a bilingual poet, and short story writer depicting a life only he knows. Julio was a student of the National Hispanic Cultural Center's Voces program. He is embarking on what promises to be a wonderful career in the field of bilingual writing and story telling.

Miranda Merklein is the publisher and editor of *Journal of Truth and Consequence*, a bimonthly arts and literature magazine based in Truth or Consequences, NM. She holds an MA in liberal arts from St. John's College in Santa Fe and a BA in political science from College of Santa Fe. A native of North Carolina, Merklein's work has appeared in literary journals, magazines and newspapers throughout the US. Currently she is pursuing a PhD in creative writing, hoping to one day make a living as a poet.

Deanna Sauceda Messenger has been writing most of her life, but this is her first piece of poetry or fiction to be published. The bulk of her writing is done at KRQE News 13 in Albuquerque, where she is an anchor. Deanna was born in Denver, Colorado and studied Journalism at Colorado State University. She came to New Mexico in 1989. Deanna took a four year sabbatical to work at Intel as a spokesperson and media manager for Colorado and later, as a project and marketing manager for Intel Community Solutions. Deanna is very happy to be back in journalism and back in New Mexico.

Brion Milar is a writer and poet raised in northern New Mexico. He lives on his family farm in the Santa Cruz Valley. He has written poetry most of his life and following retirement he began working on a collected work entitled, *CANCION DE NUEVO MEJICO*. This collection tells the story of New Mexico's history and culture through the centuries in poetic form.

Merimee Moffitt came to NM in May of 1970 in a shiny green Chrysler with some Viet Nam vets, two dogs, and one other woman, bringing whatever she could fit under the seat. She and her traveling companions drove from Portland to El Rito where she fell in love with the hills and skies and wells and los rios pequenos and her son's father, a good looking desperado if she ever met one, and she did--several. Those were the days. Look for her upcoming book of stories: "*Free Love, Free Fall*" to be published somehow by somebody soon.

Carol Moldaw is the author of four books of poetry: *The Lightning Field,* winner of the FIELD Poetry Prize, *Chalkmarks on Stone, Through the Window,* which was also published in a bilingual edition in Istanbul, and *Taken from the River.* A recipient of a Lannan Foundation Marfa Writers Residency, a Pushcart Prize, and a National Endowment for the Arts Creative Writing Fellowship, Moldaw lives in Pojoaque, New Mexico, and teaches at Stonecoast, the University of Southern Maine's brief-residency M.F.A. program.

Jon Paszkiewicz is a writer, spoken word artist, writing coach and poet from Albuquerque, NM. A member of the Albuquerque Slam Council, Jon has been involved with Poetry Slam nationals since 2005, and currently competes and lends performances to local schools.

Mitch Rayes was born in Detroit in 1958, the son of an Irish nun and a Lebanese bomb-maker. His home in Chiapas was seized by armed indigenous rebels in 1994. He married Dona Sinkevicius at the bottom of a sink hole, and they currently reside on Albuquerque's west bank with their two kids Nick and Sirena. Check out Mitch's website at www.mitchrayes.com

Jonathon Rollins has a Masters degree in astronomy and after spending a few years lecturing at the planetarium of the National Air & Space Museum, recently returned to school to pursue a PhD in astrophysics. He has published articles in *Inside Kung-Fu* and *Black Belt* magazine, as well as short stories in *Once upon a World* and *The Alibi*.

Lori Romero is a published poet and fiction writer who has served as Artistic Director of Friends & Artists Theatre Ensemble in Los Angeles. She is co-founder and co-editor of Cezanne's Carrot, a Santa Fe-based online literary journal (www.cezannescarrot.org). She currently resides in Santa Fe, New Mexico. Ms. Romero's first chapbook, *Wall to Wall*, was published by Finishing Line Press. Her short story, *Strange Saints*, was a semifinalist in the Sherwood Anderson Fiction Award and her short screenplay won the Manhattan Short Film Festival's Scripts and Screenplay Competition. Her poetry and fiction have been published in more than sixty journals and anthologies, which include *Copper Nickel, flashquake, Citizen 32, Quercus Review, Plum Biscuit, Mystic River*

Review, Edgar Literary Magazine, Poetry Motel,Pebble Lake Review, and *Mindprints* (upcoming). She was recently nominated for a Pushcart Prize.

Adam Rubinstein founded Destructible Heart Press in 2000. He's pretty sure he's been writing longer than he can remember. When he's slacking on his Destructible Heart duties, he works as a fledgling design consultant at Culture Lab. His poems have been published in numerous magazines and literary journals you've never heard of, and he has performed at more than 50 venues around the U.S. and Canada, many of which it's far more likely you have. He holds a BA in Performance Poetry and Visual Literature from Hampshire College and dreams of one day returning to the gardens of academia for an MFA, with Hell on his heels.

Miriam Sagan teaches creative writing at Santa Fe Community College, edits the e-zine "*Santa Fe Poetry Broadside*" (sfpoetry.org), and is the author of numerous books. Forthcoming in 2007--*MAP OF THE LOST* (poetry, UNM Press) and *GOSSIP* (essays, Tres Chicas Press).

Nico Sahi is a thirteen years old living in Corrales, NM. Not counting school assignments, he started writing poetry about a year ago. He has written some pretty bad ones, mainly about his crazy friends, who have inspired many a poem. Sahi loves writing and performing poetry and hopes to keep doing it for a long time to come.

Tony Santiago is a husband and father who won three consecutive Albuquerque City Slam Championships, followed by the Santa Fe City Slam Championship. He then took a year off from national competition, only to return the next year as Albuquerque's Haiku champion. In 2004 he became the first poet in history to drop out of a national competition in order to speak out against the overly competitive attitudes he had witnessed over the years. An award winning actor, comedian and DJ, Santiago has proven himself capable of winning any style of slam, be it political, literary, hip-hop, funny or deeply personal. Despite this, he prides himself most on his role as father.

Albuquerque poet, Elaine G. Schwartz, lives with her husband, Daniel, and Purr'l the Postmodern Pussy Cat. Her work has appeared in a number of publications including, *the Harwood Anthology, Central Avenue, New Mexico Poetry Tangents Internet Poetry Page, Poets against the War Internet Anthology* and an *Anthology of Monterey Bay Poets*. Prior to moving to Albuquerque in 2005, she organized a number of poetry events, including a multimedia Poets for Peace gathering in Santa Cruz, California. She is currently exploring New Mexico, as well as learning basic Quichua from her two-year old grandson, Kihua Daniel.

Jeanne Shannon's poetry, short stories, and personal essays have appeared in numerous small-press and university publications. She has published three full-length collections of her work and several chapbooks. She is editor/publisher of The Wildflower Press in Albuquerque.

Daniel (Danny) Solis started writing poetry at the age of five and has been called the Poet Laureate of Albuquerque. He's been a part of two National Poetry Slam championship teams, and has won numerous individual titles. His work has been anthologized widely, most recently in the Spoken Word Revolution. He was Festival Director of the 2005 National Poetry Slam in Albuquerque, New Mexico.

Linda Sonna is an author, poet, and essayist. She lives and teaches creative writing in Taos, NM and San Miguel de Allende, Mexico, and is Professor of Counseling Psychology at Yorkville University. See www.DrSonna.org.

Arthur Sze is the author of eight books of poetry, including *Quipu* (Copper Canyon Press, 2005) and *The Redshifting Web: Poems 1970-1998* (Copper Canyon). He is currently poet laureate of Santa Fe.

Sal Treppiedi was born in Brooklyn, New York in 1963 to Italian immigrant parents. He has lived on both coasts, but now calls New Mexico home, where he is married to Debbie, a wonderful woman with a beautiful soul, and his amazing 13-year-old daughter Calle, a budding poet herself. After many years in the music business, Treppiedi became an educator, working as a middle school language arts teacher for the past 13 years. He has written in one form or another for most of his life, but following a painful separation and divorce, he stumbled upon his first poetry slam at RB Winnings in Albuquerque. Although he performs sporadically, Treppiedi is currently working on a manuscript for his first chapbook, and plans to release it from captivity in 2007. In the meantime, visitors can access his website at www.freewebs.com/burquepoet/.

Kayce Verde was raised in Black Mountain, North Carolina and was inspired by the presence and history of Black Mountain College. In 1994 she went to San Miguel de Allende, Mexico to pursue writing and studied with the Emmy award-winning writer, Gabriela Bernard. She then moved to Taos, New Mexico where she studied poetry with 'Annah Sobelman. In 1999 and 2001 she attended the San Miguel Poetry Week and in 1999 was accepted into the Squaw Valley Community of Writers. She has had work published in *The Practice of Peace, Chockcherries, The Studio Potter, Hey, The Simple Vows Anthology*. She has been the featured reader at the S.O.M.O.S. Summer Writer's Series, The Art House in La Paz, Mexico and the St. Andrew's College Writer's Forum. Currently she is working on a book of poetry and a book collaboration with her artist husband, Gary Smith.

Israel Wasserstein received his MFA from the University of New Mexico in 2006. He was born and raised on the

Great Plains, but currently resides in Albuquerque, where he has grown used to green chile and waking with a view of the mountains. His poetry and fiction have appeared in *Flint Hills Review, Blue Mesa Review, BorderSenses, Iota* and elsewhere.

K.M. White was born in Minnesota, but has lived in New Mexico for thirty years. She retired from nursing after working as an RN for more than 25 yrs. And has been writing poetry for years but have focused more intently on it recently. She is also working more on art projects. This will be her third year studying herbal medicine, and she loves gardening; vegetables, herbs, flowers - all of it. A lot of the inspiration for her poetry comes from the natural world, its seasons and cycles, and from the creatures that inhabit that world with us.

Kimberly Williams teaches writing and literature full-time at San Juan College, where she is also the director of the SJC Poetry and Prose Project. In 2004, she was a recipient of a NEH grant which allowed her to travel through Central America and Mexico writing poetry. Some of the poetry that came from this trip has been published on thedrunkenboat.com. Kimberly is a former Case Poetry Prize winner, selected by the late Robert Wallace. She resides with her three year-old son, Andrew, and their two silly cats in Farmington, NM, where they enjoy the magnificent Four Corners sunsets nightly.

Rochelle Williams is a writer and photographer living under the spell of southern New Mexico. Her poems, short stories and photographs have appeared in *Lunarosity*, *writeronline*, *The Ink Spot*, *Chokecherries*, *The Eldorado Sun*, and *Lifeboat*, *a Journal of Memoir*.

Liza Wolff is a clinical social worker working primarily with Mexican immigrants in the field of trauma. Originally from Atlanta, GA, she currently lives in Albuquerque where she tries to write, read, hear and gobble up as much poetry as possible.

Rachelle Woods first soaked in a hot spring in the Jemez in 1985. Six years later, she stopped wandering and settled in Santa Fe to be close by. She co-hosts monthly Open Poetry and Poets for Peace readings, a writing group, a contact improv dance jam, and is a winner of the Southwest Literacy Center's Discovery Award.

Christina Socorro Yovovich writes, teaches, and studies in Albuquerque, New Mexico.

NM Poetry Tangents is a coalition of poets working together as a community benefit organization to promote literacy, especially through poetry media, and encourage the growth and unity of the literary arts, both page and stage, within the state of New Mexico. NM Poetry Tangents organizes events, publications and festivals, while its members volunteer within the schools and various agencies, organizations and charitable foundations. Our mission is to ensure the growth of the literary arts and literacy within the community, while fostering self-expression and activism through the arts for youths and adults alike.

NM Poetry Tangents exists on the web at http://nmpoetrytangents.com and can be reached at NM Poetry Tangents, 23 Longview Drive, Tijeras NM 87059 by mail. We offer free monthly writing workshops, an online publication and resources for local artists, a consistently updated calendar of events and volunteer services and performers for community events and workshops. For questions about events or to contact us for readings and workshops, please visit the website or contact us at tigerbrighttiger@yahoo.com.

Zachary Kluckman , Chairman of the Board